Praise for *Be Transformed*

"Working side by side with John for three years in our substance abuse program, I watched him pour his heart into helping my counselees gain freedom from their addictions. His book is of inestimable value, because it illustrates what is necessary to overcome self-destructive behavior and live a life that is more Christ-like. I heartily recommend *Be Transformed* to anyone serving others through ministry."

-- Malcolm R. Lewis, MD, substance abuse counselor

"I can't believe how much I have underlined. . . .When quoting John's words to a member of Alcoholics Anonymous, he responded, 'Finally, someone understands me.' "

-- M. O. Farmer, President, American Business Capital

"Powerful! The Holy Spirit is behind *Be Transformed*. It will open your heart to receive the profound transformation God has in mind for us all!"

-- G. Gustoffson, author of *The Adventure of Worship*

"I have read a book that I know will positively impact my life. . . . Important insights for faith-based ministries. I am so impressed with your work."

-- J. Casillas, Executive Director, MB Project

"Studying *Be Transformed* should be a required part of our recovery program."

-- Counselee in faith-based substance abuse program

BE TRANSFORMED

New Life Awaits

JOHN ROBIN MURPHY

Rock House Way Press, LLC
PO Box 187
Brentwood, TN 37024-0187

Copyright © 2007 by John Robin Murphy

Rock House Way Press and colophon
are trademarks of Rock House Way, LLC.

For information regarding quantity
discounts, please contact:
Rock House Way Press at 1-615-370-4795 or
visit www.rockhouseway.com

Cover designed by Brian Dominey

ISBN 13: 978-0-9788715-0-5
ISBN 10: 097887150-2

Unless otherwise noted, Scripture quotations were
taken from the *Amplified® Bible*, Copyright © 1954,
1958, 1962, 1964, 1965, 1987 by The Lockman Foundation. Used by permission. (www.Lockman.org)

Dedication

To Beth, with whom I am unspeakably blessed to be one.

Acknowledgements

My love and gratitude to my wife Beth Murphy for her tireless support, editing, and proofing. Without her, there would be no book.

My love and appreciation to my other enthusiastic partner in Christ and in counseling, Malcolm Lewis, and to his precious wife Virginia.

Thank you to Melany Klinck for being a great sounding board and editor.

I am grateful to Virginia Lewis, Deese Bearden, Otis Farmer, John Casillas, Gerrit Gustafson, Lynn Scarola, Bernie Butler, James Ackerman, Curt Masters and Randy Hearon for their diligent review of the manuscript and for their thoughtful input.

Guide to Scriptural References

All numbered endnotes refer to scripture references located at the end of each chapter.

Unless otherwise noted, scripture references are from the *Amplified Bible,* a translation that explains and expands the meaning of words in the text by placing amplification in parentheses and brackets and after key words or phrases. This system of translation allows the reader to more completely grasp the meaning of the words as they were understood in the original languages. As you read these amplified passages, note that:

- Parentheses ( ) signify additional phases of meaning included in the original word, phrase, or clause of the original language.
- Brackets [ ] contain justified clarifying words or comments not actually expressed in the immediate original text, as well as definitions of Greek names.

Contents

~

Introduction   vii

1.   One Man's Transformation   1

2.   Breakthrough   17

3.   The Missing Message   39

4.   Transformation   59

5.   Semper Fidelis   79

6.   A House Divided   91

7.   A Heart Restored   107

8.   The Truth about Lies   129

9.   "Love Me More"   145

10. The Power of Humility   157

11. Let the Transformation Begin   171

Introduction

Because God has given me a life worth living, I have loved Him since my conversion to Christianity in 1982. He has healed me and freed me from bondage, such that I could never repay Him. Thankfully, all He wants is my love, acceptance and worship. From my healing has come a desire to see others set free. This desire is similar to the feeling you experience when you first affirm the Word in your heart and want to share the powerful Truth with everyone. I carry and have carried many titles and labels in the world, but all I really am is a lover of the Lord, who shares His desire to heal others and set them free from bondage.

The purpose of this book is to advance the Kingdom of God. As always, the theater of war for this battle is the human heart. In this case, it is specifically the heart of Christians. Through my ministry experiences with inner city substance abusers and everyday Christians, and through God's ongoing work in my own heart, I have been allowed to see how the battle for the heart is waged.

This battle underlies everything we struggle with in our lives. Whether we are addicted to drugs or shopping, it is a heart issue. If we can't seem to keep the weight off after multiple diets or we can't stop yelling at our spouse, it is a heart issue. If we feel like a loser when our team loses or if our sense of self-worth is based on our financial worth, it is a heart issue. If we feel we cannot connect with God and our spiritual growth is stalled, it is a heart issue.

The heart is the epicenter of our well-being and our struggles. That is why the victory that God wants is in our hearts. During my last 24 years of Christian ministry, many key spiritual principles that predict the outcome of the heart battle have become clear to me. These principles have been confirmed repeatedly as God has patiently advanced His kingdom in my own heart, transforming places of darkness into places of light. I have also observed this same process as it has occurred and failed to occur in the hearts of those I have loved and counseled.

When the Lord sets you free, the powerful desire to see others set free becomes a driving force in your life. It has taken me to places in my heart concerning relationships and places of ministry that were unimaginable. His freedom is a gift that has made me a new person in Christ. It is my hope that sharing my walk of heart transformation and the truths that I believe God has revealed to me will provide new hope and new energy to your pursuit of the abundant life God wants for you. May this humble effort spark you to battle for territory in your heart for His glory and your blessing.

Chapter One

One Man's Transformation

For I endorse and delight in the Law of God in my inmost self [with my new nature].

Romans 7:22

Stupid, ugly, unlovable and worthless best describe what I believed to be true about myself as an eight-year-old. I was the youngest boy of four siblings in a family that had no regard for God. The circumstances of my life introduced and reinforced these lies, producing a heart surging with the emotional pain of self-hatred, isolation, depression, emptiness and even rage. To manage these intensely negative feelings, I started early in life pursuing worldly comforts and sought affirmation in whatever form I could find it. Because these lies had been perpetrated by people, most people became either the focus of my hatred or merely prospects to fill my emptiness.

During elementary school and high school, these early beliefs became self-fulfilling prophecies, confirmed by how I was treated and how I performed as a student. With a heart and mind working overtime to manage my feelings, staying focused on school was nearly impossible. Attending school was a miserable experience, as my grades each year were just barely adequate to avoid being held back. Trying to overcome the intensely negative feelings arising from my poor self-image and many failings drove me to seek comfort in food. By the age of 12, my weight had ballooned to more than 200 pounds. My shame, fueled by the obvious disapproval of most everyone in my world, resulted in me trying to eat my way to a state of numbness.

Desperate for acceptance, approval, and love, I was an attractive target for those skilled in providing very conditional acceptance to satisfy their own relationship sickness. Seizing the opportunity to spread his brokenness, an older boy in the neighborhood introduced me to sexual perversion through pornography when I was 10. Since it provided a strong feeling that crowded out my pain, it was added to my strategy for survival.

Friendships were rare in my adolescent world. Interaction with peers was usually in the form of conflicts with other boys. Overweight and unathletic, I was an easy target for their harassment. The random and unexplainable attacks were the most frightening. I vividly remember the day a gang of boys I had never seen before jumped out of some bushes along a dirt road to attack me with a hail of rocks and dirt. Another time, a child spit in my ear simply to entertain others nearby. The situation wasn't much better at home, as sibling encounters commonly took a toll on my limited self-esteem. Unpredictable hazing during my adolescence established my life pattern, characterized by just trying to survive one episode of cruelty after another.

As a high school sophomore, I encountered a new tormentor in the form of a teacher and football coach who held a grudge against me. His condemnation of me was born out of my refusal to make my 6-foot, 260-pound body available to help him achieve his coaching aspirations. He retaliated by beginning each class with a public proclamation of my worthlessness. The same "tonnage" he wanted to exploit on the football field became the means of attacking my self-esteem. He actually stated that my only value in life would be to "sit around and melt (so as) to bring down the cost of lard." My last day in that school came when a football player and I were taken to the principal's office for talking in class. The football coach was summoned to mete out the punishment. The football player was lightly paddled; I received an abusive beating.

In later high school years, I was targeted from a different direction by someone who saw opportunity in my emptiness and my desperate search for kindness, acceptance and love. The summer before my senior year, I had a job where I met a young, attractive woman who worked as an assistant nurse at a local hospital. She was approachable and friendly and seemed to have a genuine interest in me. We began dating soon after our first meeting, even though two others suitors were competing for her attention. I was quite infatuated, perhaps somewhat obsessed with her.

Our platonic relationship was the focus of my life for six months. Before I returned to boarding school that Christmas break, she announced her plans to have surgery for "female problems." A week later I called home from boarding school to ask my mother to send flowers to the hospital. She told me that my "girlfriend" had undergone a sex change operation and was actually born a man. My father, a physician in that hospital, had discovered the truth, further straining our difficult father-son relationship. The news delivered a profound shock to my soul, leaving me with a broken heart and a tidal wave of shame. I struggled not to question my sexuality or to let the depth of my depression render me completely unable to function.

After that event I really didn't like most people, and was especially suspicious of women. The remainder of my senior year in high school was largely a battle to retain my sanity. Feelings of victimization, anger, betrayal, suspicion and bitterness enveloped me in a blanket of depression so thick that it was often physically difficult to stand erect. To survive this condition, I believed the only solution was to pursue every mood-altering activity or substance the world offers a troubled soul to cool the fire that rages within. This "medicating" became the first priority in my life. I would do practically anything to crowd out my feelings.

My freshman year of college brought with it the disorienting news of my parents' divorce and access to more and new medicating activities to get relief from my emotional torment. I was profoundly wounded and empty and focused solely on stuffing the world's idols into my personal darkness. Throughout college and into the first few years of my career, my gluttony included drinking. Soon I was in the habit of getting drunk three or four times a week. My weight approached 300 pounds. Coarse speech grew into a constant stream of four-letter words. Obsession with drinking and female companionship led to routine intoxication and sexual encounters that left me empty and more deeply entrenched in my shame.

Accomplishment seemed a viable way to deal with my pervasive sense of worthlessness. In my early teen years, I decided that I would feel better about myself if I could become accomplished in something. Years were spent trying to master photography, playing the flute, piloting aircraft, lifting weights, competing in racquetball, and pursuing other competitive or creative distractions. I reasoned that if people would praise me for my accomplishments, then my sense of worth and self-esteem would be restored. So I worked to achieve all those goals and more. The compliments came, but relief did not follow. At this point, no amount of positive attention or praise could fix me.

As I worked through my list of accomplishments and saw that each had failed to bring me the sought after relief, I kept hoping that my next achievement would be the answer. And it was this hope that kept me going. By my mid-20s, there seemed to be only one thing left to try. In deluded desperation, I convinced myself that this goal would fill me with self-worth and peace. This ultimate goal was to own my own business. So I bought controlling interest in a small community advertising company. It didn't last a year. I lost my entire investment and became embroiled in a lawsuit.

Owning my own business was literally the last thing on the list. Since everything that I tried had failed to bring me fullness and peace, I didn't know where to turn. This latest failure brought me to a new depth of hopelessness and a sense that my life truly had no value, no happiness, and no point.

The day I realized there was nothing left to put my hope in, I was with a woman friend whom I knew to be a Christian. I had forbidden her to discuss her beliefs with me. I had known a few vocal Christians through work and hated them all. Any references to God, Christ, or Christianity by Christians enraged me. One of my favorite topics of discussion was the non-existence of God, which I had long assumed to be true. To prove my point, I had actually cursed God in front of people I knew to be Christians and dared Him to strike me down if He existed.

Now in a place of hopelessness, I shocked my friend and in some measure myself when these desperate and somewhat sarcastic words came from my lips, "Tell me about this God thing." The next two days were spent learning the liberating truth of the Gospel. It became clear to me that the living God and His Son Jesus were the answer to the hole in my soul. By the end of the third day, the Lord God Almighty had become a fixture in my heart as I declared the truth of His Son at the age of 26. That dear friend has been my dear wife since 1983.

On one level, my search had been based on my desire to relieve my emotional pain. But on a deeper level, it was also a search for the meaning of life. I had never previously considered that this had anything to do with God. It was only when I'd reached the end of my list of accomplishments and was looking for a scrap of hope that I was able to hear the truth.

Even as an unbeliever, I knew enough about Christian values to realize that nearly all of my medicating tactics were sinful. Somewhere inside, I probably also knew that any acknowledgement of His existence threatened to cut off my medicating behavior. To me, that was a death sentence. I later learned what would be required in order to truly live. The man I had become would have to die.

Upon committing to follow Christ, some changes in my life were immediate. Foul language and my habit of getting drunk three to four times a week ended, and my self-esteem began to grow. My priorities switched to reading Scripture and Christian books that furthered my understanding and commitment. The first years of my faith were characterized by excitement about the truth I had found and trying to believe that God's promises for an abundant life could apply to me.

However, something curious happened after about five years of being a Christian. The familiar misery from my old life began to return. Certainly my Christian foundation was intact, but some of the initial excitement about becoming a Christian had begun to fade. In its place, I began to feel that familiar anger, depression, and sense of limited self-worth. I had definitely not fallen back to my pre-Christian condition, but I was hurting.

I sought the help of a Christian counselor. Five years later, I stood healed from many of the effects of a lifetime of abuse, which had continued to plague me for years after my profession of faith. The most profound healing came from forgiving the people who had hurt me. I depended heavily on God's help to get through it. Along with that forgiveness came freedom from a lot of emotional pain.

The most notable burden lifted when the Lord led me to deal with my relationship with my dad. I had worked to put a good face on it, but every now and then I would say something that made it clear to all that I was still angry with him. On occasion, he would do something that would set off a firestorm of negative emotions and bring on some type of inappropriate behavior. Fortunately, the Lord led me to have the same grace for my dad that God has for me. Through a simple prayer of forgiveness and repentance, that relationship was made right by the power of God. Soon I experienced feelings of love for my father I had never known. What had been a strained relationship perpetuated by my judgment and unforgiveness became one in which I deeply cherished him. I also came to appreciate his many great qualities and how much he loves me. Our restored relationship has become one of the crown jewels of my faith. Breaking through on this heart issue was the cornerstone event that led me to dig into many other places of unforgiveness. Another layer of torment that had driven my more socially acceptable medicating behaviors was gone.

Taking on the Sin

Over the next seven or so years, I experienced some periods of spiritual growth, but overall, I felt there had to be more to my faith. I was spiritually dry. Prayer was difficult. I could not maintain a routine of studying the Word and resisted doing the Lord's work. Praising the Lord in song was refreshing spiritually, but it was about all the presence of God I could muster. I seemed to be stuck and was grieved by this.

I wanted a more meaningful relationship with the God who had done such profound work in my life. One day I was looking through an old briefcase and found a simple silver cross that my wife, Beth, had given me. I hadn't worn it for very long after receiving it, but sensed that maybe wearing it again would remind me to think of Jesus as I felt it tap against my chest over my heart. There was no discernable change at first, but I did feel that the cross was in some small way making a difference. It was not the cross but the decision to wear it that ultimately made the difference. While I felt a bit more connected to God, there was still a great distance between us, as if loving Him from afar.

Over the months that followed, my love of praising the Lord grew. Praying came more easily. I asked God for a deeper relationship with Him, for help in breaking through my feeling of disconnectedness. My prayers and meditations led me to consider the recurring patterns of sin in my life. I became convicted that even though my life was greatly cleaned up from pre-Christian days, sin was still robbing me of a full and satisfying relationship with the Lord. This relationship block also made it impossible for me to hear His calling for me, which was something I intensely wanted to know.

Following the conviction welling up in my heart, I saw the truth about myself. As a 43-year-old man and a Christian for 17 years, there were still sin patterns in my life born out of my dark, pre-Christian years. Hidden within an apparently cleaned up life were sins I relied on for comfort that needed to be confronted. Even though my life was very Christ-focused, I had been unwilling to rid myself of remaining sins that separated me from God and squelched my desire to be more committed to Him. I had not been able to trust that God had a better way for me to live. Still dependent on the things of darkness, I turned to those places of sin for temporary escape.

As I actively pursued a relationship breakthrough with the Lord, the first barrier to be confronted was borne out of my past exposure to media. In the middle of solemn prayer, sexually suggestive images or violent scenes would invade my thoughts. Recognizing these visual impressions came from the media I was viewing, I began to seriously consider cutting out a life-long crutch – movies and television. The conviction ultimately came. Regardless of what others might need to do, it was important for me to be careful of what I exposed my heart to. It was a clear case of "garbage in, garbage out."

Repentance did not immediately follow the conviction. The life change occurred when the Holy Spirit prompted me to take an honest look at what television meant to me. The truth was that I had been strongly dependent on television throughout my life for comfort and escape. After becoming a Christian, I initially had ignored television to pursue my faith. But within a year, it had become a key factor once again. Given my obsession with TV and my reliance on it as a child, it's not surprising that I returned to it after the excitement of being a new Christian was no longer enough to separate me from my negative emotions. Even after being relieved of the torment of unforgiveness, the draw to medicate by watching television was strong. It was a high priority idol, and I behaved as if I loved it.

As an adult Christian, it was obvious that doing something other than watching television was a wise choice, especially if it were God-focused. However, I still spent many nights watching television for hours. Regret would always follow, along with a recommitment to myself to do better next time. For many years, that night never came. The pattern was predictable: Visual enticement always led to giving in, followed by regret and shame. That matches the workings of any sin or behavior that is out of control.

Traveling for work was the worst. The TV in my hotel room typically stayed on for hours, often tuned to programs with enough sex and violence to grieve the Spirit dwelling within me. Finally, the Lord led me into deep thought that unraveled this pattern of sin, revealing that television had become a significant idol in my life. I realized I was turning to television instead of the Lord for fulfillment. Of course there was no fulfillment in that black box, and it always served as a distraction from my need for God-centered fulfillment.

In examining the way I watched television, several principles of the way sin operates in our lives were revealed to me. The first is what I call "legitimate entry." The reason to turn on the television always seemed to be legitimate. My favorite excuse was that watching the news made me a better-informed Christian.

The "brilliant rationalization" began each night with the feeling I had worked hard all day and had earned the right to some mindless relaxation. In reality, I was rationalizing the second pattern, which I call "returning to the areas of sin." I'd developed a routine in which fifteen minutes of watching news led to spinning channels with the remote, sometimes for more than an hour. In hotel rooms where I stayed while on the road for business, my channel-spinning lasted from dinner until bedtime.

My third insight was that this seemingly superficial, harmless ritual was actually a search for flesh or violence. This relentless search for a peak of excitement that is so engaging that it removes you from your world is what I call "spiking." Think of it as the first moment of feeling, that surge you experience when your eye transmits a stirring image to your brain. There is an immediate emotional spike as the image excites you and crowds out other feelings.

Feeling excitement is not the problem. The problem is having an unconscious obsession to search for excitement spikes that grieve the Spirit and cut you off from the Lord. I found that most of my time alone in front of the TV was really spent looking for sexually suggestive images or violence – a desire to return to pornography and the hate that remained in my heart. It became clear that as long as I was under the influence of movies and television, there would be no victory over the 10-year dry spell in my relationship with the Lord. There was no hope of achieving a deeper connection with God while I pursued the idol of worldly excitement. I made the decision to no longer go to movies or watch TV.

The sin pattern was broken with prayers of repentance and a firm resistance to being drawn back. However, the temptation was still strong, and that surprised me. All I knew to do was to believe in God for His power to resist temptation. This brought up a troubling question: If I truly wanted to do the Lord's will, why did I still have this strong desire to return to sin?

Getting to the Heart Issue

During a season of wrestling with this question, I had an opportunity to watch some videos about a ministry that was focused on helping people break free of their sin patterns through confession and prayer with a fellow believer. The ministry targeted sexual immorality, unforgiveness, fear, and involvement with the occult. My first reaction to the ministry was that I already had enough shame about my sins and did not particularly want to expose my sinful self to other people. Surprisingly, my heart shifted dramatically when the leader explained that a person's spiritual gifts and calling often become clear when sin patterns are brought into the light and broken. Furthermore, the very sin that someone struggles with is likely to be related to the focus of his or her calling.

I sensed that this ministry had discovered something significant. The conviction to dig in hit me the next morning during a business meeting with 10 people gathered around a conference table. During someone else's presentation to our foreign business partners, I responded to an urge to flip open my portfolio. I wrote down every sin in my life I could think of that could be blocking my relationship with God and giving Satan legitimate access to torment me. The list filled a page. The places within me that needed attention were not related to fear or the occult but to the wounds left from unforgiveness and inappropriate sexual behavior from my pre-Christian days. These were the burdens from which I wanted to be set free.

The desire for freedom brought on one of the most difficult challenges of my Christian life. Because the process involved spending time in confession and prayer with a couple of other believers, it required exposing my sins to someone else. Scripture certainly validates this approach, but my shame filled me with dread. Memories of public ridicule from peers and hazing scenes from childhood consumed my mind.

When the time came to actually receive the ministry that was required for my personal freedom and for later ministry training, I was overcome by shame and wanted to run screaming from the building. The battle that raged within me was a spiritual war between the darkness that did not want to yield and the spirit of God, which called me to a place of holiness where I could rely on Him for all I needed. A dear brother in Christ saw my struggle and came over to pray for me and gave me a comforting bear hug. Strengthened by his love and committed to the course of freedom, the session began. Two hours later, after praying to God for forgiveness of my sins and forgiving those who had hurt me, I experienced a new level of peace and freedom.

I was amazed to find that not only had a spiritual burden been lifted from me, but a physical one had fallen away, as well. Standing erect literally took less effort. For the first time, I had a personal understanding that the yoke of Christ is a far lighter burden than the one of unforgiveness and sin that had weighed me down. I was truly in a new place, thanks to the power of confession and repentance. The fear and reluctance about unveiling my sins to others seemed insignificant compared to the relief and joy that resulted from getting another part of my spiritual house in order.

Many things have changed since that time. Overall, my relationship with the Lord continues to improve, as does every aspect of my life. What is most exciting is my growing desire to pursue God through His Word and to advance His Kingdom. The greatest blessings have been a significant improvement in my prayer life and a new level of discernment of His Word. No longer were these practices guilt-inspired drudgery.

As for my calling, it has become clearer to me. Those things that once caused me the most anguish are the basis of the work that the Lord has called me to do. He has given me a hunger to minister to others, particularly to men. For the past three years, I've been working with male substance abusers in a local rehab program. I have seen my willingness to share my struggle with common sins convince men to examine and confess the sins in their own lives. They are drawn to understand their own legitimate places of need and confront how those needs lead them to the illegitimate and dark things of the world.

My Spiritual Revelation

The purpose of this testimony is to let you see the restorative work God has done in my life and to convey the perspective from which I approach all ministry, particularly to those needing a radical life change. My experiences with substance abusers, combined with years of working through my own issues and providing ministry in marriages and in emotional healing, have provided the context in which I believe the Holy Spirit has given me critical enlightenment.

The revelation is that true change only comes when we are transformed at our core, at our heart level. This transformation is available to all, but it does not automatically commence with our salvation. We have to take action to clear the way for heart transformation. Such transformation starts with the willingness to build a new life to whatever extent is required for real change. *All efforts that do not begin by clearing the way for change will result in change that only occurs on the surface.* Should that happen, we become imposters at war with our hearts as we try to maintain a new veneer. That veneer will ultimately be worn off from the inside out.

Each step along my path of transformation has required humility, honesty, and a longing to become closer to God. By any measure, the payoff has been worth the effort. I have been freed from the bondage created by the behaviors I adopted to medicate my self-imposed torment. I've discovered that it is indeed good to allow the Kingdom to take ground in our hearts. It truly brings us closer to the One who created us and loves us perfectly. Perfectly.

Of course, heart transformation requires us to not only love the Lord, but also to love His law. If we conform to His will as expressed in His law, we will be free of the torment that drives us to self-destructive behavior. Forgiveness and humility are the cornerstones of getting right with the Creator. But all God's laws apply. All of the impurities and ungodly offerings of the world can establish bondage in our life, and we are warned by the Bible not to give in to these temptations.

However, I want you to know that you can be the person that God wants you to be. His work in my life proves that transformation is attainable by all. His way truly is easier. I would have been free much sooner if I had sought His solutions rather than my own. I understand the allure of a quick drink, a quick hit, or a quick peek. But I also know from experience that we cannot heal our souls by feeding our flesh. Healing our souls requires humility, obedience and change.

Transformation will challenge your resolve, and Satan will always resist it. However, Scripture promises that you can defeat him:

> *And they have overcome (conquered) him by means of the blood of the Lamb and by the utterance of their testimony...*
> Revelations 12:11

With that in mind, I humbly submit this testimony to you. Be encouraged that when you invite the Lord into the dark places in your heart, sin patterns will yield to His peace and freedom. He will fill the legitimate need you have with enduring wholeness and fulfillment.

Chapter Two

Breakthrough

For those whom He foreknew [of whom He was aware and loved beforehand], He also destined from the beginning [foreordaining them] to be molded into the image of His Son [and share inwardly His likeness], that He might become the firstborn among many brethren.

Romans 8:29

God Has Done it Again!

There has been a breakthrough, and that breakthrough has been in me. Actually, there has been *another* breakthrough. The feeling is familiar because He has done it before. This time, the memory is vivid and my thoughts about what it all means are intensely clear. The astonishing awareness came in the midst of the mundane. I was leaning on the kitchen counter, striking the familiar pose of "it's dinner time and I'm here to eat," when I was frozen by sudden awareness that God had given me a gift I thought unattainable. I had never considered that I might escape the dark self-condemnation that had always haunted me after making a humiliating mistake.

Earlier that week, I had lost all composure in a confrontation with some of my son's teenaged friends while they were guests in our home. My ranting was made worse by my total failure to remain in "adult mode." I could just imagine how the story of my door-slamming, finger-pointing rage was going to be told to their parents. For me, it would be hard to imagine a more embarrassing and public mistake. In the past, a dark cloud of self-condemnation would have engulfed me. This time it was different. There was no trace of that painful recrimination within me, even though difficult conversations and humble apologies were soon to come. I had received a precious gift of freedom from self-condemnation.

I tried to communicate to my wife, Beth, the shock of realizing and experiencing unexpected freedom and peace in the midst of this relationship calamity. "Beth, you know what is so amazing about all of this?" I asked, in a somber tone of surprise. "I have peace. And I am not beating myself up. I can tell that it really is okay, because for the first time in 48 years, while I am convicted that I made a mistake, I am equally convicted that it's all right. I feel intact, instead of being ravaged by self-condemnation. I am a human being who makes mistakes, and I know that I am acceptable anyway. Any other view I've had of myself has been a lie. It is not true that my worth is based on always getting it right or on anyone else's opinion of me."

Freedom from Living a Lie

That lie had been a predictable source of torment my entire life. But that day I felt free and at peace, even facing the prospect of having to apologize to the parents of my son's classmates, conversations in which I would have to own up to my failures and ask for forgiveness. In spite of the dreaded task ahead, I stood in the kitchen, calmly acknowledging my failure to Beth, but full of peace.

This was a momentous breakthrough of miraculous proportion. For the first time in my life, I really understood the Lord's truth that I am fully loved by Him, even though I am imperfect and have no righteousness on my own. In this condition I stand equal with all humanity.

Normally it would have stung to recognize the depth of my need, but instead, it was a relief. I felt like a different person, not the guy who had overreacted by yelling at his son's friends just a few days before. I liked the new me and was very grateful that I would not have to live that other poor soul's life any longer. God had rewired another part of my heart and made me a new person. God had completed another increment of my transformation. I actually had more peace, because a chunk of self-righteousness had been broken off and was no longer available to condemn me for my mistakes.

The most compelling confirmation of my new existence was the absence of any desire to medicate or separate from my feelings. Normally, such an event would have caused intensely negative feelings. Those feelings, in turn, would have launched a temptation to suppress my anguish with food, television, obsessive reading, or one of many other solutions the world offers.

The Old Ways

Before becoming a Christian, I would have escaped from my feelings through more conspicuous self-destructive behaviors, such as a night of drinking that lasted until early morning. My intense self-condemnation would subside, only to be replaced with shame brought on by the previous night's alcohol-induced behavior. In turn, that shame would trigger another run to the bar. I repeated that cycle frequently in those days. Later, as a Christian, God's many healings lessened the intensity and occurrences of those negative feelings, and I migrated to more socially acceptable "antidotes." But the purpose was the same — giving in to the temptations of the world to cool the pain in my soul.

God's Way

So what was different this time? Why was I not obsessed with my failure? Why did I not stick my head in the fridge for a little comfort food? The only logical conclusion was that *I* was different. Following that awareness came the recognition of God's familiar pattern of transforming my heart. God had peeled off another broken layer of my heart, leaving me changed and grateful for His work. I had been rewired, essentially becoming someone new. I was no longer that other person. Perhaps I was only incrementally different, but it was nonetheless another progressive step along God's growth path for my heart.

In Romans 12:2, Paul calls us to be transformed by the renewing of our minds. God has truly transformed me, layer by layer, over the past 24 years. The gift of more freedom has come in the process. It was this new freedom from self-condemnation I sensed in the kitchen that night. Because I had recently recognized, confronted and repented of self-righteousness, the door was open for God to change me. I received the blessing from God that caused my heart to be a little more like His Son's as I conformed to His laws.

Looking back over my life, especially at the person I was at the time of my conversion to Christ, it is clear that I am truly a different man. That old heart, characterized by wounds and worldliness, no longer defines me. Many things that motivated and led that person have no power over me today. A powerful truth is that I have not just developed a pleasing veneer that's constantly warring with my heart; instead I have actually become someone new. Great peace comes from my improved condition. My heart is much more aligned with God and who I want to be on the outside.

The Gift of Transformation

Transformation is a calling and a gift from God that is strangely overlooked in many Christian circles. Yet, it is a fundamental calling for all believers. Christians frequently wonder what their calling or purpose in life might be. I believe it is clearly stated right there in the Bible: *Be transformed.*

Is it not incredible to you that all Christians are called to be transformed into His image and to have the heart of Christ? It definitely struck me that way, and I remember the day it happened. One day while thinking about the Father's perfection and His love for us, I was startled by this new understanding. God is the greatest and is above all else; therefore the highest blessing He can give us is the opportunity to be like Him. Envision the praise-worthy Creator of all things, looking over creation and deciding that the greatest gift He can give us, after reconciling us to Himself through Jesus Christ, would be to make us like Him. Not to be Him, but to be *like* Him. For He knows His freedom, His love, His peace, His power, His joy, and His glory. And we are called to conform to His image and share in His divine nature. It is consistent with the personality of the loving Father to want to give us the exceedingly best gift He can give us. How surprising is it that He desires us to be like Him? Scripture is clear that we reap God's promises as we become less like the world and more like Jesus. God's desire is for us to be blessed. The promises that bring the blessing are realized as our hearts increasingly resemble the heart of Jesus.

The focus of my entire Christian life has been to embrace the promises of Scripture and to activate them in my life. Only through the three-year experience of ministering to men in a drug rehabilitation program have I finally realized that my journey is one of transformation. I now see that this is a foundational call of God. We are not intended to casually plop ourselves down in the salvation seat and cruise through life claiming the promises of God and expecting the abundant life. We are called to become someone new as we internalize the Truth and engage in the actions of living as Christians. As Paul wrote to the Ephesians:

> *Strip yourselves of your former nature [put off and discard your old unrenewed self] which characterized your previous manner of life and becomes corrupt through lusts and desires that spring from delusion; And be constantly renewed in the spirit of your mind [having a fresh mental and spiritual attitude], And put on the new nature (the regenerate self) created in God's image, [Godlike] in true righteousness and holiness.*

Ephesians 4:22-24

My understanding of this call came through an earnest desire to help those men at the drug rehab program get free of their addictions and have a new life. In the process of trying to help them achieve permanent freedom, I realized the progressive change underway in my heart and the freedom that was active in my own life. Then the truth in the words that I spoke to them *worked to affect my heart as well.*

At the same time, I recognized that the obstacles facing these addicted men were monumental. Most were my brothers in Christ, who had put their trust in the Lord, but still struggled with addiction. The challenge to get free and stay free of drugs or alcohol had been largely unattainable for them. Some had been through as many as 20 other programs by the time they came to ours.

As part of my role there, I spoke to all 70 men on

the last Tuesday of each month. I always prepared by asking the Lord, "What do you want me to tell them tonight? What can I say that will help set them free from their bondage? What do you have for them?"

At first, I shared my own testimony of freedom from my days as an unbeliever and showed them the spiritual principles in Scripture that were at work in each situation. Some time during the first year, however, it was obvious that I was getting nowhere. The men were grateful and seemed to hear the messages, but as they graduated from the program, a grievously high number of them returned to their addictions. The rehabilitation process had provided them with the opportunity to get sober and to dig into the Lord's truth so they would be well prepared to live a successful life. It provided a critical step in their recovery, because there is no hope without first becoming drug free and then having God's truth poured into a sober, believing mind. Yet they needed something more to achieve victory in the power struggle with their addictions.

God's Answer

On one of those Tuesdays, the Lord revealed to me the only answer: Transformation. He reminded me of the transformation that had occurred in my life. It was an example of what they and all of us must do in order to be free of any behavior we can't control.

When I asked God what to tell the men that night, I had a strong impression that played out in my mind as this "conversation:"

John, why don't you still weigh 300 pounds?
"I don't know. Why?"
Because that is not who you are.
"What do you mean?"
Your heart does not drive you to eat at the level it

takes to sustain that much weight. I have rewired your heart. I have transformed you. You are not that person anymore.

I immediately knew this was God's answer for what the men needed. It made so much sense. It also tracked as the answer to many of the other patterns of behavior that no longer ruled my life because of His transformation.

From as early as I can remember, I struggled with being overweight. At the age of 11, I even went off to fat camp for the summer. I will never forget reading the application my father, a physician, filled out. He described me as obese. That hurt! This was in 1967, long before one-third of the U.S. population was considered obese. I was a standout. My weight problem was a source of embarrassment for my dad and shame for me.

I had definitely eaten to medicate my feelings throughout my life. Some people wear their emotions on their sleeves. I wore mine under my belt. Eating was how I coped with pain and frustration. I probably would have weighed even more had I not played soccer. At 260 pounds, I was perhaps the heaviest first-string varsity soccer player in school anywhere. My weight eventually topped out at slightly less than 300 pounds when I was a college sophomore.

I had tried every conceivable diet through the years with no lasting success. The familiar pattern was to lose weight after exerting Herculean amounts of self-control, only to gain it back, and then some. I tried countless methods to get free of my weight problem, but never could achieve a lasting victory. It was basically a "white-knuckle" endurance approach to weight loss.[1]

I was never free from the desire to overeat in those days because I was never free from believing the lie that it would ease my emotional pain. Food really didn't provide comfort as much as it distracted me from the discomfort of my emotional struggles. Although the results of overeating may be more benign than drug addiction, my battle with weight helped me understand the bondage of addiction experienced by the men in the drug program. I wanted God to show me how to help them.[2]

The results of God's work in my life showed me the way. Since becoming a Christian, I have been transformed. I have sustained a 60 to 70 pound weight loss and have no desire to eat the way I used to. This is not because I use some self-help routine to manage food temptation. It's because my changed heart harbors less emotional pain and doesn't drive me to medicate it. I have a new heart. I am a new person. Just as the Scripture called me to become a new person in Christ, I realized that each of my struggling brothers in the program needed to become a new person in order to be free.

It was not enough to be free of drugs for a time because for these men the problem always came back. What they needed was the same thing you and I need, to be free of an irresistible level of temptation and desire to sin. We all experience temptations, but most are the run-of-the-mill variety that we can easily put out of our minds. You might entertain a fleeting thought of robbing a bank to pay the bills, for example, but it is so inconsistent with your heart and your values that you would not find it difficult to resist such an urge.

This is about temptation that effectively keeps us in bondage because we can't consistently resist it. These sin patterns have a measure of control over us, which at the very least can make us miserable or, when full blown, have the potential to ruin our lives. Bondage is not restricted to particular sins, so it does not really matter what the issue is. *If we are unable to stop doing something, we are in bondage.* While we all have a sin nature that tempts us, it is our failure to control a sin that indicates the presence of a heart issue driving that behavior. And if we can't get ourselves to do something we need to do, such as look for a job or make a tough call to a child's teacher, it is a heart issue that has us bound up.

A Struggle That is Common to Man

While working with these men, I realized that they are just like me. They are simply in a different place on the continuum of the Lord's transformation.

In this Christian drug program, God's promises are taught and discussed at great length, along with the blessings and spiritual realities that come with being a child of God. In fact, most of these guys believe that if they stick to the routine of pursuing the Lord through prayer, regular devotion time, and attending church, they will do well on the outside after graduating from the residential program. But they rarely do. Many simply can't stay free of the addiction that is ruining their life.

Why do they fail? They fail for the same reason that we all fail if we think that spiritual routines alone will solve our problems. These routines alone do not lead to the death of the old self. If there is no birthing of an addiction-free person within the heart, there will be no transformation. And if we do not experience transformation, it is because we do not really want it.

What we really want is to avoid the consequences of our behavior. It is symptomatic of our culture to demand a quick fix to all problems. We resist denying ourselves the things we want and refuse to change our lives to solve our problems. We want pills, self-help programs, or positive self-talk to help us live a more abundant life, in spite of how we may choose to run that life. It is a vain attempt to achieve the quality of life promised by God by responding to the call of our flesh. There could not be a more profound disconnect. The abundant life of God is not available through reliance on the world. However, it *is* available through the transformation God has called us to.

We All Just Want to be Fixed

The "I just want to be fixed" sentiment so prevalent in our culture was never more apparent to me than when I was listening to a man tell his story about how he had gone through multiple rehab centers, but was unable to get free of his addiction. He was looking for the same solution most of us want. He wanted the Lord to fix him. Most of us really don't want to change; we just want the Lord to take away the nagging, recurring sin pattern or sleepless nights while giving us more money, stopping the migraines, healing us, or fixing our spouse. Our fleshly hearts seem to say: "Just make it go away. Don't ask me to change. Just fix my problem."

It reminds me of a situation that occurs everyday somewhere in this country, when a teenager ends up in jail. The teenager just wants out. His one call is an anxious plea for his parents to fix the problem. That plea comes with promises to change and do whatever it takes to get free. The parents must decide whether to bail him out and rescue him from his pain or to let him spend at least a night in jail, which could spark a beneficial heart change that only suffering can bring.

Few people would not share the teenager's desire to be rescued. But God does not bail us out. He does not choose to alter the effect of breaking His Laws. He is no more likely to remove the discomfort of sin for Christians than to change one of His physical laws. No matter how much we pray, God will not change the boiling point of water for our singular convenience. That does not mean he causes our suffering. While God establishes the consequence of breaking His Laws, we are the ones who break the laws. So He does not bring suffering upon us, we do.

God's desire is that our suffering will cause our hearts to change. Hearts *can* be changed, particularly when motivated to end suffering. But first we must discover what it is about our hearts that opposes God's will. In Romans 8:28, God promises to work all things together for good in the lives of those who love Him. That "good" can come from any event in our lives that changes our hearts. It does not mean that God will bail us out of the predicaments brought on by our sin or remove the pain caused by our sin. That would not be consistent with His goal for us to be Christ-like.

God knows that freedom from suffering follows our taking an action to become a new person who is no longer controlled by the temptation to indulge in ungodly behavior. If our suffering causes us to change our hearts to reap the benefit of living within His Law, that is another way in which the Romans 8:28 passage is fulfilled.

The Solution is a New Life

The church has largely succumbed to this fix-me-quick culture. The truth of transformation and what is required to become a new person in Christ is absent from many pulpits. Instead, many churches today support a "salvation equals abundant life" form of spiritual immaturity. The promises of God are pored over and poured out on Sunday morning crowds. "This is who you are in Christ," some pastors say. They follow this with a list of God's power and promises with little or no mention of the conditions upon which those promises are made.

By the end of such a message, many in the pews are expecting the abundant life to be theirs. However, in exactly seven days, everyone floods back into the sanctuary needing another power talk after a week much like the last one. They need another reminder of the promises that never seem to come true for them. They might wonder,

"Why wasn't last week any better? All the promises are there in the inspired Word of God, but it just isn't happening for me. I'm not being fed. I pray and have devotions, but there is no change." Some might be able to exist longer than others on the excitement of God's promises, but eventually reality kicks in. Along with it comes disillusionment and familiar patterns or problems that seem insurmountable.[3]

As I reached out for God's answer for the men in the program, the freeing truth became clear for me and for them. *There is no change without transformation.* Each week will be much like the last unless we become someone new over the course of that week. If the Holy Spirit doesn't make a new creation out of my heart, then I will work off the same platform as before. Every time a certain stimulus comes into my world, I will react the same way. And I will feel the same shame one more time for the way I deal with my pain.[4]

That describes a life in bondage, and that is not the life God has for us! How could that be the plan of a God who desires to transform us all into His image? This is a God who created us to share in His divine nature and be full of His light and His love, to have a life free of bondage, full of peace and contentment, with no anxiety about life situations.

In Romans, it says:

For if you live according to [the dictates of] the flesh, you will surely die. But if through the power of the [Holy] Spirit you are [habitually] putting to death (making extinct, deadening) the [evil] deeds prompted by the body, you shall [really and genuinely] live forever. For all who are led by the Spirit of God are sons of God.

Romans 8:13-14

Remember that Christ came to save us, heal us, and

deliver us. Salvation is all about His work and our faith. But
the healing and deliverance that can only be accomplished
by the working of God's power does take effort on our
part. This is not like trying to achieve righteousness
through "works," but we must exert a certain diligence to
see the truth about ourselves and act upon it. It is about
understanding our role as Christians and living accordingly.
During the journey, if we are willing to allow our minds to
be transformed by the precepts of Christ, God evolves us
into someone new. The resistance we all feel is an unwill-
ingness to readily accept truth that threatens who we are
and what is important to us. The truth will challenge the
things that drive us. It will challenge the way we lead our
lives, from where we live to what we read, even the essence
of who we think we are and what we like to do.

You will know the truth and the truth will set you free.
John 8:32

Yes, it will set you free, if it is allowed to challenge
you and change you. The old self cannot survive the im-
plementation of God's truth. And it is only as we realize
and conform to God's truth in our lives that we can receive
His power and promises.

Peter expresses it this way:

For His divine power has bestowed upon us all things that
[are requisite and suited] to life and godliness, through the
[full, personal] knowledge of Him Who called us by and to
His glory and excellence (virtue). By means of these, He has
bestowed on us His precious and exceedingly great promises,
so that through them you may escape [by flight] from the
moral decay (rottenness and corruption) that is in the world
because of covetousness (lust and greed), and become sharers
(partakers) of the divine nature. For this very reason, adding
your diligence [to the divine promises], employing effort in

exercising your faith to develop virtue...

2 Peter 1:3-5

This Scripture speaks of God's power and our diligence, not "name it and claim it" godliness.

Active Spiritual Laws

There is definitely something we need to do to receive the blessings God has promised us. Some would say they are doing it by living their Christian values, but they still feel stuck and unable to get closer to God. Others may feel they are on the right track spiritually even though an unwanted behavior has gotten control of their lives. So what is to be done?

We must understand that *the promises of Scripture are not available apart from the commands of Scripture.* An example of this is Paul's statement:

We are assured and know that [God being a partner in their labor] all things work together and are [fitting into a plan] for good to and for those who love God and are called according to [His] design and purpose.

Romans 8:28

Thus, we can only expect all things will work to our good *if* we love God. The reverse is also true. If we do not love God fully, all things will not work to our good. We cannot expect to receive the promise if we fail to fulfill its undetachable requirements.

Here is another example of a promise of power and authority from James that Christians, including me, commonly quote:

So be subject to God. Resist the devil [stand firm against him], and he will flee from you.

James 4:7

Again, the promise comes with conditions. To succeed in making Satan flee, we must subject ourselves to God and exert effort. Otherwise, we will not have the power to resist Satan.

The Inner Working of God's Laws in Our Lives

If we want victory over bondage, we must embrace God's clear mandates in Scripture. For instance, Paul explains to the Ephesians God's will for how to manage anger and the consequence of not doing so:

When angry, do not sin; do not ever let your wrath (your exasperation, your fury or indignation) last until the sun goes down. Leave no [such] room or foothold for the devil [give no opportunity to him].

Ephesians 4: 26-27

Is it not implicit that if we let the sun go down on our anger, we are opening ourselves up for Satan to get a foothold? And we can assume Satan's foothold will be pretty negative. Let's say it manifests as depression. Even the secular world recognizes that unresolved anger leads to depression. Do we deal with the torment of depression by simply claiming the abundant living promised by God or do we obey this scripture, thereby removing Satan's foothold?

In the parable of the unmerciful servant, the king forgives his servant for a debt he could never repay. However, when the servant is asked to forgive a lesser debt owed to him by another, he refuses. When the king hears about it, he turns the unforgiving servant over to the torturer. What does that mean to you and me? Christ revealed the spiritual principle of the parable when he said:

> *So also My heavenly Father will deal with every one of you if you do not freely forgive your brother from your heart his offenses.*
>
> Matthew 18:35

Remember, this is also a promise of God. Can we simply claim peace and joy as promises from God while ignoring this one? If we are unwilling to forgive someone who has asked our forgiveness, we are promised torment.

The critical point of both passages is that there is something we can do or leave undone that gives Satan legal access to torment us. We can provide Satan an opportunity to wreak havoc in our lives. We can actually open the door for the evil one, who searches the earth to find those he can kill, steal, or destroy. And we know Satan goes through every door into every heart that he has the right to enter. The parable also warns us that God will proactively turn us over to Satan if we withhold our forgiveness from another.

Does just the knowledge of those two principles set us free, or are we required to take an action? Are we free from the consequences of unforgiveness by knowing what to do or by doing it? Only by choosing to forgive do we reject the desire of our flesh to hold a grudge and thereby close the door to Satan's torment.

Some believers who desire freedom from the temptations of Satan recite the same passage of scripture the men in the program commonly proclaim:

> *. . . Resist the devil [stand firm against him], and he will flee from you.*
>
> James 4:7

So why do believers operating under the authority of this verse fail in their efforts to resist Satan? And how does this truth relate to the other two spiritual truths from Ephesians and Matthew where we are warned that unforgiveness allows Satan a foothold and prompts God to turn us over to the tormentor? It is plain that there is more to getting free than the knowledge that Satan will flee when you resist him.

Resisting Satan from leading us into a sin *and* allowing him a legal foothold to torment us are conflicting propositions. How can you operate in your God-given authority to resist Satan and at the same time be subject to his right to have a foothold in your life and torment you? Clearly, you cannot resist Satan when you have given him authority to have his way with you. So if you are stuck in a sin pattern and rely on the scriptural promise to "resist the Devil and he will flee" to gain your freedom, it will elude you.

You are suffering from a heart issue that puts your spiritual house in disarray. That condition is totally consistent with the spiritual laws God has set in place. The condition of our heart defines who we are. If we do not want to suffer from the results of unforgiveness, then we need to forgive in order to achieve a breakthrough in the quality of our lives.

If you try to practice Christian virtues but seem unable to get closer to God, or if you feel it is hopeless to change your life for the better, be encouraged, because the Lord has the solution. If you humbly seek His truth and desire the freedom that comes from being transformed into His image, you will not be disappointed.

The New Life Requires the Death of the Old Life

As you apply truth to your life and receive freedom, you may experience discomfort as you "kill off" the old person. The process will challenge you in every way. It will challenge your pride, your superstitions, your self-righteousness, and your very life as you know it. You will need to literally die to parts of yourself if God is to make you into someone new.

As Paul challenged the Colossians:

> *So kill (deaden, deprive of power) the evil desire lurking in your members [those animal impulses and all that is earthly in you that is employed in sin]: sexual vice, impurity, sensual appetites, unholy desires, and all greed and covetousness, for that is idolatry (the deifying of self and other created things instead of God). It is on account of these [very sins] that the [holy] anger of God is ever coming upon the sons of disobedience (those who are obstinately opposed to the divine will)*

> Colossians 3:5-6

Dying for the cause of freedom has a long, honorable, heroic, and *fruitful* tradition, begun in its purest form by Christ Himself. He came to save us from our darkness knowing that we would kill Him. He loves us so much that He died to establish our freedom from death. Moreover, He came to save, heal, and deliver us from bondage. Now it is our turn to operate in the divine power that He made available. We can exchange the darkness that we struggle with for more of His light and thus become inwardly more like the God in whose image we were made. Christians have been transferred into the Kingdom by Christ's sacrificial act of defeating our sin and reconciling us to God. Therefore, we can expect to live in freedom from bondage and to receive increases in peace and joy if we operate in *all* of the truth of God's Kingdom. I believe transformation is the key to the life we all want, and that life bears more than a coincidental resemblance to what we are promised and called to as Christians. As I observe the process of transformation in my life in context with and in contrast to most of the men in the rehab program, the power and necessity of transformation are compelling.

While I didn't know what to expect to learn from counseling men in this program, I certainly did not anticipate realizing that we are all the same. I did not expect to conclude that the spiritual process that gives them freedom is the same one everyone else needs. I did not expect to learn anything new or to be nudged along in my personal transformation. I did not expect my life to be changed as I tried to bring change to others in Christ.

The calling, process, and blessings of transformation are not frequently discussed, at least not in my church history. This book is written in the context of my testimony and ministry activities both within and outside of the inner city drug rehab program. These experiences have brought understanding that I believe will be helpful to you whether you struggle to be free of addiction or bad habits, to keep the pounds off, or to achieve more peace and abundance in your Christian life. May the Lord bless you with what he has shown me.

Supporting Scripture References:

1. "Such [practices] have indeed the outward appearance [that popularly passes] for wisdom, in promoting self-imposed rigor of devotion and delight in self-humiliation and severity of discipline of the body, but they are of no value in checking the indulgence of the flesh (the lower nature). [Instead, they do not honor God but serve only to indulge the flesh.]"   Colossians 2:23

2. "They promise them liberty, when they themselves are the slaves of depravity and defilement—for by whatever anyone is made inferior or worse or is overcome, to that [person or thing] he is enslaved."   2 Peter 2:19

3. "Therefore, my dear ones, as you have always obeyed [my suggestions], so now, not only [with the enthusiasm you would show] in my presence but much more because I am absent, work out (cultivate, carry out to the goal, and fully complete) your own salvation with reverence and awe and trembling (self-distrust, with serious caution, tenderness of conscience, watchfulness against temptation, timidly shrinking from whatever might offend God and discredit the name of Christ)."   Philippians 2:12

4. "Now if [all these things are true, then be sure] the Lord knows how to rescue the godly out of temptations and trials…"   2 Peter 2:9

Chapter Three

The Missing Message

I fed you with milk, not solid food, for you were not yet strong enough [to be ready for it]... but even yet you are not strong enough [to be ready for it], For you are still [unspiritual, having the nature] of the flesh [under the control of ordinary impulses].

1 Corinthians 3:2, 3

It is Time for Solid Food

I am writing this on Monday, January 2nd. Yesterday, our family had the uncommon experience of attending church services that actually fell on New Year's Day. The message we heard, however, was very common. It is one that tends to pervade sermons during this season, promising an improved life as the new year gets underway.

As the preacher framed the message, a familiar theme emerged. It was a challenge for us to live a truly Christian life. The logic this Sunday was just as valid as every other time I have heard it. But as the message developed and concluded, there was little new information presented about how to actually accomplish the challenge.

The essence of his appeal was that although we have

received salvation through our faith in Jesus, we should not stop there, satisfied with the knowledge that we will be with God when we die. We are not to put God's "seal of approval" in our wallets to be whipped out at our death like a movie ticket to gain entrance into the Kingdom. The pastor encouraged the congregation to take action, to "press in" to their faith, to live out their faith every day. I couldn't have agreed more. Everything he said was absolute truth. Then why don't we see sustained improvement in the lives of those who hear this message?

The pastor stated that the way to achieve a more fulfilling life in Christ is to recommit to Bible reading and daily prayer. For a helpful study system, he directed us to a book available for purchase in the narthex. It would lead all takers through daily devotions and Scripture passages, guiding the diligent through the whole Bible in a year. How could one take issue with that proposition? Certainly reading the Bible in a more disciplined fashion and praising God more often would positively affect anyone's Christian growth.

Yet isn't that the same challenge issued here at the beginning of last year and issued at the beginning of many years in many churches? And hasn't the church really been saying that same message, with or without occasion, as long as it has been in existence? It is essentially the same type of theme promoted by any institution that wants its participants to affect a beneficial life change. It reminds me of the high school principal at the beginning of the school year telling all the students to study harder. Is it likely that the students will work any harder as a result? Or will they be more inclined to exert the level of effort they always have based on what kind of student they are in their heart?

So why do pastors feel the need to continually urge their congregations to press in? Because the pastor can see that his flock would be greatly blessed by a deeper life of faith if they would respond to the call. Also, the fruits of a congregation in diligent pursuit of God's call would be vastly different than those produced by the people now filling his pews.

On the face of it, there is nothing wrong with the call to improve our lives by reading more Scripture and spending more time in prayer. However, considering how few people actually accomplish sustainable change, it's clear something is missing from that message.

It's just not that easy to create significant change in our lives. An obvious example of that is the custom of making New Year's resolutions. If a poll were taken of people who have made New Year's resolutions, which of the following commitments to life improvement do you think is most likely to be broken?

❖   Lose weight

❖   Stop drinking

❖   Spend more time with the kids

❖   Treat my spouse better

❖   Stop smoking

❖   Stop looking at pornography

❖   Read my Bible more

❖   Pray more

❖   Get more sleep

❖   Eat right

❖   Get more exercise

The answer to the poll question is that most of them will be broken, and virtually no New Year's resolution results in a truly changed person. Oh, a few of us may be able to maintain the desired behavior for awhile, but the underlying purpose of the resolution — to affect a true life change — will usually elude us. What we yearn for is not to just control the behavior, but to be the kind of person who *effortlessly* keeps their weight in check, or doesn't smoke, or always eats right, or has no urge to yell at the kids, or never looks at pornography, or . . . pick your resolution. We witness a characteristic in someone and decide that's how we want to be. There is nothing wrong with witnessing a behavior in others that sparks a conviction to change. But then we try to copy the behavior, and we find the effort it takes to be like that person consistently is more than we can sustain. Usually our hearts reject the grafted-in character trait, like an organ transplant gone bad, and we are left feeling discouraged.

You can't achieve lasting change with temporary or superficial solutions. You can take enough medicine to stop coughing, but you still have the cold. You can make yourself stop drinking, but still be an addict. Instead of trying to emulate the *behavior*, we need to emulate the *heart* that drives the behavior.

It is the heart's condition that drives the sin pattern and thwarts our spiritual progress. Religious logic may tell us that simply behaving like a Christian *should* make the difference. But that's true only to the degree our hearts allow it. Our hearts hold the truth of who we are. So you could say that the "true us" blocks who we want to be.

So how do we unravel that conundrum? My experience with the guys in the substance abuse program exposed the answer, and it was confirmed by what I sensed to be true about my own heart. But I had to fail in my attempts to help them before I could see it.

I typically spoke to all the men in the program once a month at their Tuesday evening chapel, as I mentioned earlier. In this endeavor to bring them the freeing truth, God showed me that my message was not what they most needed to hear from me. For the first six months or more, I spoke about all the promises of God and explained how reliance on these promises could free them from their addictions. I passionately presented my belief that a new life without addiction depended on pressing into a relationship with God, on accepting His promises as true in their lives. I sounded exactly like the pastor who addressed my family at the New Year's Day worship service. I encouraged them to stay focused on Jesus. Pray all the time. Meditate on the Word.

Finally, I realized that the words I said to the men were like those of all the others who spoke to them. Furthermore, it was evident that this advice was not producing the breakthrough success these men needed. Like ministers and preachers all over the world, I was operating on the false premise that anyone can achieve sustainable improvement in their quality of life simply by reading more Scripture, engaging in more prayer, or doing more service. This is commonly described as "pressing in." And those who adopt a "pressing in" routine may be blessed by a closer relationship with God, but, too often, they fall short of the truly changed life they seek.

So if a God-centered routine does not change lives, what does? Why had the men been unable to achieve success over their addictions by changing their behaviors? And why are we not able to fulfill our own New Year's resolutions? I know I never have.

Our Heart is the Key

The answer is in our hearts. Victory eludes us because we are trying to be someone we are not. If we have no heart-level desire or inclination for a behavior, doing it conflicts with who we are. We can discipline ourselves to start new good habits and resist bad ones, but most of us can only do it for a time. The true self grinds against such imposed habits, and the heart always wins.[1]

Thank God that we are actually able to change! In fact, our hearts can turn completely around to embrace the truth we have previously rejected. An example is my own conversion to Christianity, which came after 26 years of denying God and resenting His people. What's more, I am living proof that we do have the power to reject the lies of this world and allow God to transform our hearts.

The vital message that is so often absent from the pulpit and from most other sources that promote life change is that transformational change is an *inside-out* job. Instead of trying to act like someone who doesn't have a shopping obsession, we must become someone who is not drawn to shop obsessively. Instead of medicating our emotional pain, we need to address the underlying cause, the core, the root, the heart of the problem.

Our hearts are not changed simply by stopping the behavior. But our behavior will change when we change our hearts. Since our hearts represent our true selves, we need to become someone else if we want to change our behavior permanently. I appreciate and admire how now-sober people participating in Alcoholics Anonymous (AA) continue to call themselves alcoholics. It is an important reality, because it tells the truth about their heart. They know what they are dealing with. They are still alcoholics in their hearts. They have stopped the behavior but are not kidding themselves about what their heart would drive them to do if they were not participating in AA meetings and routines.

Yet, God wants us to be free of our self-destructive behavior, and that means becoming someone new. Of course, it is critical for one to be sober in order to have any chance of success in the transformation required to be free of addiction. The results of 12-step programs such as Alcoholic Anonymous or Narcotics Anonymous are vital, but sobriety is not the same thing as being free from addiction, nor does it resolve the question of why people abuse substances. That answer is wrapped up in who we are. In order to be free, we need to alter who we are and become someone new.

Here is another way to look at the dynamics of the situation. Let's pick on obsessive TV watchers this time – another one of my former medicating activities. It is interesting to note that when I became a Christian, I was immediately convicted that television was consuming my life. My first solution was to put the remote control in an inconvenient place, hoping to break my habit of automatically spinning channels after dinner each night. I quickly realized that was not going to work, so I unplugged the television and demoted it to a closet dweller, where it stayed until I moved several months later. During those months I had little interest in watching TV.

However, when Beth and I married and began setting up our first house, we put the television in a prominent place in the den with the assumption that its pull on me had disappeared. Even though I had not watched it for months, I picked up right where I had left off and began watching obsessive amounts of TV. This continued for a regrettable 15 years before I finally dealt with the problem on a heart level.

This kind of behavior relapse was exactly what I witnessed in the drug program. The men would be sober for seven months, expressing little or no interest in getting high by the middle or end of the program. But on the day of graduation or soon after, many would be right back in their addiction, because the heart issues that drove their addiction had not been resolved.[2, 3]

In confronting my heart issue during my 40s, I came to understand that watching television separated me from my emotions. The more intense the feelings delivered to my brain by violence or strong sexual content, the more distant my negative emotions seemed to be. My constant search for spikes of intensity was similar to the experiences substance abusers described. The excitement of the feeling from a brief scene would begin to wear off as it aged in mere seconds, spurring me on to the next one. In working with substance abusers, I found the same principle at work in their lives. First they are enticed by one drug, then, when it is no longer enough to separate them from their reality they begin to use more frequently or to use stronger drugs. I heard countless stories of consuming addictions that started with a few beers, then escalated to include marijuana, heroin, crack cocaine, or methamphetamine.

These men's emotional pain, just like mine, was the root cause of their obsessive behavior. Yet, the common approach to treating the obsessive behavior was to focus on eliminating the symptoms, rather than going after the sickness at the heart of their problem.

The missing message for these men and for all of us seeking to eliminate destructive behaviors and sin patterns from our lives is that we need to become someone new. And that means dying to who we are. We cannot just proclaim our Christian beliefs and expect all of the promises of God to be instantly realized. Christianity has the answers to whatever your heart struggles with, but it is not an effortless, quick fix. And claiming Christ as our savior is not a way to duck the consequences of our behavior.[4]

This missing message is actually the missing link between accepting Christ and living the abundant life. Access to the abundant life and all the promises of Scripture beyond the rewards of salvation are realized through the process of becoming more Christ-like.[5, 6]

Jesus charged His apostles to do more than simply make disciples of all the nations. Consider the entirety of what Jesus said to them. (Added emphasis is mine.)

"*Go then and make disciples of all the nations, baptizing them into the name of the Father and of the Son and of the Holy Spirit,* **Teaching them to observe everything that I have commanded you,** *and behold, I am with you all the days (perpetually, uniformly, and on every occa-*

*sion), to the [very] close and consummation of the age. Amen
(so let it be)."*

Matthew 28:19-20

The phrase in bold is the second part of what many
Christians call the "great commission," and it speaks to
God's desire that we live a life that is consistent with His
commands. Notice the wording of the phrase. The disciples' priority is not to teach God's commands but to teach
people how to *observe* His commands. Winning a convert for
Christ and then moving on is not what Jesus has called us
to do. The disciples are told to teach converts to *observe* His
commands so that they, too, may receive all of the rewards
and promises of a God-centered life.

One of the rewards for observing God's commands
is to be included in Christ's Kingdom family. Here in the
gospel of Mark, He takes the opportunity to reinforce the
importance of doing the Fathers will.

*And looking around on those who sat in a circle about Him,
He said, See! Here are My mother and My brothers; For
whoever does the things God wills is My brother and sister
and mother!"*

Mark 3:34-35

Church Appeal

To become new in Christ means to die to self. It is
an uncomfortable process, full of humility. Most people
would rather just get fixed. I would say that if someone
wants a quick fix, he needs to go elsewhere. However, there
is nowhere else to go. Getting truly fixed is not available
anywhere else. Think back to Chapter 1. I tried everything I
thought the world had to offer to fix my profoundly
discontented life. Nothing worked. If you truly want to be
free of a self-destructive behavior, you must become

someone new. There is no alternative.

So why don't we hear this message from the church or the self-help world? Well, it's not very appealing. It is especially unattractive when compared to the false promises of the world, which are so much more inviting. Which message would draw more people to a church?

This one?

"Come to our church and we will show you how to live the blessed life of Christianity. One simple statement of faith and weekly participation in our Sunday routine is the key to the Kingdom. You won't have to change your life or give up the things you most like to do. Besides, we are nice people and you will enjoy your time with us. You will also be glad to hear our building campaign is now complete, so we will have our own gym in six months."

Or this one?

"We know that a life without Christ is miserable. It is where we all were, and well remember what it is like. Come to our church, where we believe that the life you really want, the life that is gratifying and peaceful, comes from the process of being transformed into a new person. The life that your heart really wants will only come from dying to yourself."

"Humility and self-denial will be required to have your new life with Christ. Many of the things that seem vital to you now will be rejected by you as self-destructive. You will have to repent of some things you now love to do and cannot imagine living without. In fact, you will be expected to love God more than anything else. All of this will come from heart-work and will involve an internal struggle that will be uncomfortable at times. There may be times when you will find yourself stuck and unwilling to move on. On some nights you will struggle with the truth of who you are and you must

summon great humility to break through. There will be days when all you will have to hold on to are God's promises, while nothing soothes the flesh that must die for the new person in Christ to emerge. By joining our community, you are choosing heart change over endlessly battling the symptoms of your life struggles." [7, 8]

"Change will not come quickly, and may actually take years for your new life to fully emerge. And by the way, you are never done. You will enjoy the fruits of your transformation all along the way, but since the goal is to be transformed into the image of Christ, you will never get there in this life. Keep in mind that the new person you become will probably begin to drift away from your current relationships toward others who are on their own path of transformation. There is no guarantee that you will be able to or even want to continue in relationship with your current social group. However, you will grow to love God more, and God's love for man will grow in you. Others on this transformation path will love you with a purity rarely found." [9, 10, 11, 12]

"You will be drawn into ministry alongside fellow Christians, who through their love of God will share His love of man with you. As a result, you will experience some of the most rewarding and effortless ministry work of your life. It will fill you with a deep, no-strings-attached gratification. Although you don't know us, we will love you through the process. You will always have faith in His promises, and His presence will grow stronger as your heart reflects His image."

The call to transformation in the second message is off putting for a culture that wants a quick and painless fix. Ours is a culture that wants to believe there are three simple steps to achieving emotional, spiritual, or financial nirvana. The propaganda claims a new, redeemed, restored, and fun life is easy to achieve. This lie takes us down an appealing road, but one that is ultimately and literally a dead-end.

Also in our Christian culture, we don't like to talk about sin, especially when the conversation highlights our current behavior. Yet, it is our sin behaviors that stand in the way of God's call to our transformation. It seems that it has become too uncomfortable for Christian leaders to challenge the sin behaviors that cause suffering and stall our transformation. They are comfortable talking about sin in the context of salvation, but not in calling believers to a transformed life. Many Christians fear that to challenge a sin in others is to condemn or judge them.

I suspect that part of the problem is the sin word itself. The word "sin" has been used incessantly as the "battering ram of salvation." It has taken on a kind of repulsive "dirty word" stigma beyond its meaning.

I will never forget the first time I heard a fire-and-brimstone preacher warn all the "heathens" in the audience:

> "Now for all you *sinners* out there who are everyday practicing the work of the *Devil*, through acts of *vile sin*, there is no hope for you without Jesus. You *sinners* who reject the love of God in favor of the *vile* and *disgusting* acts of the flesh, and you *backsliders* who have turned your backs on God and returned to your *shameful* life of *sin* – REPENT! Give your life to JESUS! Or, all uh ya' are gonna BUST HELL WIDE OPEN!"

I admit that when I first became a Christian, the word sin did kind of get stuck in my craw. However, as I grew in faith, I realized the word "sin" really means "breaking God's rules." With that perspective, it was easier for me to look at my sin as an act arising from a rebellious nature, rather than as an act of someone who loves nasty, antisocial behavior. In fact, the word sin as used in the Bible is sometimes best defined as *lawlessness* or *lawbreaking*. Separating the sin "stigma" from every wrongful act, prevents me from heaping so much shame upon myself that I want to deny the truth about my sin. Reducing the amount of negative emotion tied up in the word also makes it easier for me to give or receive input about matters of sin.

Pastors admittedly feel the pressure to preach a Sunday message they believe the congregation wants to hear. How often do you hear a sermon that deals with divorce, materialism, pornography, or sex outside of marriage, for example? These types of sins are common to Christians and most do not want their socially acceptable sins or hidden sins to be challenged. Preaching transformation would be like addressing all of them all at once. All sin keeps God at arm's length and has to be addressed when confronting the heart condition that motivates these behaviors.

Another reason we don't hear the transformation message is that most self-help groups and church leaders truly believe, despite the glaring lack of results, that profound life change comes from more discipline, new routines, and effective self-talk. Many spiritual leaders may also have their own issues that stand in the way of their personal transformation. Thus, they are unable to lead others through the process. Those in ministry are as human as the rest of us and are also susceptible to the idea that quick, painless fixes work. I completely understand a pastor's temptation to default to the New Year's resolution sermon. He hopes that maybe this time it will take.

Compliance with God's Law Brings Transformation

My understanding that quick fixes are an illusion came during my fifth year of being a Christian when my "new Christian" euphoria evaporated, exposing my troubled heart. Perplexed, I sought counseling from my pastor. However, I quickly realized he was not going to be able to fix me. So I began seeing a Christian counselor. I hoped that telling my life story to a fresh face would have a different result. I was looking for compassion and wisdom that would make me "all better" and restore my Christian excitement.

The weeks of counseling sessions turned into years. While much of the wisdom and compassion I received was helpful, the centerpiece issue was that I had heart-work to do. The powerless condition of my shallow Christian life was not going to change until I actually began to live the life of a Christian. And that is true for all Christians.

God wants us to be transformed to resemble the inward likeness of Christ and share in His divine nature. As Peter wrote:

> . . . *He has bestowed on us His precious and exceedingly great promises, so that through them you may escape [by flight] from the moral decay (rottenness and corruption) that is in the world because of covetousness (lust and greed), and become sharers (partakers) of the divine nature.*
>
> 2 Peter 1:4

Obviously, a cornerstone of Christ's life was forgiveness. In contrast, the focus of my life at that time was unforgiveness. The sun had been going down on my anger for a very long time, even during my Christian years, and Satan had established the foothold warned of in Scripture.

Fortunately, God gave me the strength to forgive, and that changed who I was at a heart level, altering my life forever. Forgiveness was the transforming act that gave me a different life. Over time, the key antagonists in my life became people I cherished. The depression that flowed from unforgiveness began to ebb away. The first round of forgiving, and there were more to follow, was a watershed experience for me. It lifted me to a new level spiritually and began to yield fruit as a much-improved quality of life. Matthew was right:

> *For if you forgive people their trespasses [their reckless and willful sins, leaving them, letting them go, and giving up resentment], your heavenly Father will also forgive you.*
>
> Matthew 6:14-15

I wish that it had been made clear to me from the pulpit that we are called to be transformed into the likeness of Christ, that it is our highest priority and the wellspring from which all of the power and promises of abundance flow. It was the missing message that I really needed to hear in order to be challenged and to be made uncomfortable with my weak Christianity. I needed to be told that bitterness and condemnation do not exist in a heart that resembles Christ's. I needed to understand that if I was in church to claim the promises, but was unwilling to change my heart, I might as well stay home.

Proverbs beautifully sums up the importance of the heart in living a fuller life in Christ:

> *Keep and guard your heart with all vigilance and above all that you guard, for out of it flow the springs of life.*
>
> Proverbs 4:23

We all need to hear that the promises of God are available to those who align their hearts with His law. But we also need to be reminded that transformation is not a works-based activity either. It does not arise from service to others, but from conforming to His laws. And all of his laws are in effect all of the time. Remember that the most important law is to love God with all you are and have. Fruits will be born out of the love. Thus, the more we conform to His laws, the more we will desire to do good works, bringing with it His reward. [13]

And now the message is no longer missing for you.

Supporting Scripture References:

1. "As in water face answers to and reflects face, so the heart of man to man."   Proverbs 27:19

2. "Create in me a clean heart, O God, and renew a right, persevering, and steadfast spirit within me."   Psalm 51:10

3. "As for what was sown among thorns, this is he who hears the Word, but the cares of the world and the pleasure and delight and glamour and deceitfulness of riches choke and suffocate the Word, and it yields no fruit."
                                                    Matthew 13:22

4. "We know that our old (unrenewed) self was nailed to the cross with Him in order that [our] body [which is the instrument] of sin might be made ineffective and inactive for evil, that we might no longer be the slaves of sin."
                                                    Romans 6:6

"And having been set free from sin, you have become the servants of righteousness (of conformity to the divine will in thought, purpose, and action)."   Romans 6:18

5. "The thief comes only in order to steal and kill and destroy. I came that they may have and enjoy life, and have it in abundance (to the full, till it overflows)."
                                                    John 10:10

6. "But now since you have been set free from sin and have become the slaves of God, you have your present reward in holiness and its end is eternal life. For the wages which sin pays is death, but the [bountiful] free gift of God is eternal life through (in union with) Jesus Christ our Lord."
                                                    Romans 6:22-23

7. "And those who belong to Christ Jesus (the Messiah) have crucified the flesh (the godless human nature) with its passions and appetites and desires."   Galatians 5:24

8. And have clothed yourselves with the new [spiritual self], which is [ever in the process of being] renewed and re-molded into [fuller and more perfect knowledge upon] knowledge after the image (the likeness) of Him Who created it."   Colossians 3:10

9. "... work out (cultivate, carry out to the goal, and fully complete) your own salvation with reverence and awe and trembling (self-distrust, with serious caution, tenderness of conscience, watchfulness against temptation, timidly shrinking from whatever might offend God and discredit the name of Christ)."   Philippians 2:12

"[Not in your own strength] for it is God Who is all the while effectually at work in you [energizing and creating in you the power and desire], both to will and to work for His good pleasure and satisfaction and delight."
                                        Philippians 2:13

10. "So then those who are living the life of the flesh [catering to the appetites and impulses of their carnal nature] cannot please or satisfy God, or be acceptable to Him."   Romans 8:8

11. "But each in his own rank and turn: Christ (the Messiah) [is] the first fruits, then those who are Christ's [own will be resurrected] at His coming."   1 Corinthians 15:23

12. "But the fruit of the [Holy] Spirit [the work which His presence within accomplishes] is love, joy (gladness), peace, patience (an even temper, forbearance), kindness, goodness (benevolence), faithfulness,"   Galatians 5:22

13. "Delight yourself also in the Lord, and He will give you the desires and secret petitions of your heart."

Psalm 37:4

Chapter Four

Transformation

Do not be conformed to this world (this age), [fashioned after and adapted to its external, superficial customs], but be transformed (changed) by the [entire] renewal of your mind [by its new ideals and its new attitude], so that you may prove [for yourselves] what is the good and acceptable and perfect will of God, even the thing which is good and acceptable and perfect [in His sight for you].

Romans 12:2

A Calling for All of Us

Transformation is more than a spiritual principle. It is our core calling, our path to freedom, and our key to taking on His divine nature. It honors the Giver and advances the Kingdom in our hearts. Led by the Holy Spirit and allowed through our humility, transformation is the dynamic force that will advance you toward all that you yearn for in life. It is fundamentally what we are called to do and required to do if we want to realize the promises of the Christian life as described in the Bible. [1]

Many Christians undertake a quest to discover their

life calling. I have been one of those who have wondered
what I was put on the earth to accomplish. I always expected that my calling, when I discovered it, would be
something exciting or noble or maybe a source of riches.
Everyone wants to think they have a unique calling.
Uniqueness appeals because we all want to be someone
special. "How will God uniquely use *me* for His purpose?"
we ask ourselves, hoping that God gave some special
consideration to each of us as He was crafting us before the
beginning of time. [2]

Of course, He has. As a matter of fact, He has given
it perfect thought. Consider that for a minute. The all-
knowing Lord of truth and righteousness, the perfect and
praiseworthy Father who created all and sustains all, has
considered all things and has chosen your calling! And He
knows that His decision is perfect and right for you. So
what has He decided would be best for you? *To be like Him!*
That is the core calling for all of us.

We are called to be transformed into His image, to
take on His divine nature and to develop the heart of
Christ. Imagine how Christ and God must feel inside. They
are full of light and love and joy and peace and every other
promise that is ours in Scripture. Is it not just like the
loving Father to want His children to have what would
most deeply bless them? The very idea of sharing in His
divine nature and sharing in the quality of His existence
makes any career or worldly calling pale in comparison.[3]

And because He's a loving Father who wants to ease
us along the path to ultimate peace and joy, He has created
us all in His image. That's a pretty good start!

He has done much of the work for us. We have
been transferred into the Kingdom by the unselfish and
sacrificial act of His Son Jesus. [4]

He has put within us the Holy Spirit, which is the
very mind of God. [5]

And He has instilled in us a desire to understand

and respond to our calling. This call to transformation, to take on the divine nature of God, is extended to all Christians. When we respond to His call, the Lord, through the Holy Spirit, will guide our hearts to serve Him, and all of the promises of Scripture become real and available to us. In Peter's first letter, he tells us:

> . . . *You are a chosen race, a royal priesthood, a dedicated nation, [God's] own purchased, special people, that you may set forth the wonderful deeds and display the virtues and perfections of Him Who called you out of darkness into His marvelous light.*
>
> 1 Peter 2:9

As we progress through the transformation process, we will experience breakthrough after breakthrough on our journey to emulate Him. This is what Paul is talking about in his second letter to the Corinthians when he writes:

> *[We] are constantly being transfigured into His very own image in ever increasing splendor and from one degree of glory to another. . .*
>
> 2 Corinthians 3:18

By becoming more like Christ, we are fulfilling God's desire for us. But that only happens if we walk in a way that glorifies Him. As we emulate Him, He is honored and receives glory. Our outward actions that prove our commitment to Him bring Him glory. So as we shed worldly characteristics for more Godly traits, we are transformed from glory to glory.

Transformation Ushers in the Promises of God

The life-changing reality of this process is that with every new breakthrough along the continuum of transformation, we see the Father more clearly, and we experience more and more of His promises. [6]

Those promises are the same ones many Christians hear every Sunday but never seem to achieve. We drag into church, settle into our power pew for a shot of good news, and then head out into the world on fire again. But as we move through the next week, we act more like a dimming bulb than a raging fire or even a glowing ember. If the transformation process is not underway, very little actually changes week after week. No matter how much we may want to believe that the Father's promises are real and active in our lives, when we fail to experience them our frustration level mounts until apathy and routine set in and become the essence of our church experience. Unfortunately our church experience impacts our relationship with the Creator.

The activities we choose between Sundays are rarely benign. If we are not moving from glory to glory, then the week is typically characterized by decisions that separate us from God as we repeat patterns of sin or engage in self-destructive behavior. This weekly cycle brings more shame and more need for that Sunday shot in the arm, a shot that seems to carry us less distance each week. Attending church becomes more frustrating, and God's promises seem less attainable. Disillusionment and loss of faith can be the end of this sad trail of seemingly broken promises.

Transformation is the Only Answer

My guys in the drug rehab program will tell you that they want to receive the same promises of God that you do. But they can't seem to stay sober or drug-free long enough to bask in the glory of the Lord and feel His joy and peace. That was why I struggled to find a way to help them. I would pray, asking the Holy Spirit, "What do you have for these men? Why can't they stay free? Why doesn't it work for them to resist the Devil? Why do so many of them fall back into a life of addiction after seven months in rehab, where they abstain from drugs and alcohol, are covered in prayer, regularly study the Scripture, and are counseled by loving people?"

Many actually return to their street ways the night of their graduation from the program. This occurs even though their graduations were full of excitement and praise to God for their freedom, frequently accompanied by standing ovations and tears of joy from graduates and their families. An outside observer of any faith would be impressed by the conviction and redemption claimed in these men's lives. Yet, too many of them will return to the self-destructive behaviors that brought them to the program seven God-soaked months ago.

The reason so many relapse is that there's a big difference between transformation and behavior modification. It is the difference between creating a routine, religious or otherwise, that changes behavior and *actually being free of an irresistible urge that resides in the heart.* Consider what is more consistent with the personality of God. Do you think He would prefer you to be free of the temptation or would He be satisfied if you were simply able to control the destructive behavior? Is it really like Him to want us to redirect drug usage to a more socially acceptable obsession like eating candy or ice cream? Or would He rather see us resolve the broken places in our hearts that drives us to do things that dishonor Him and inflect suffering on us? [7]

The Loving Father is After Our Hearts

Think for a minute about the Scripture that says to look lustfully at a woman is equal to the deed of adultery. It is intended to draw our attention to the heart and discredit the practice of willful sinning that can be atoned for through some Old Testament ritual of sacrifice.

God is in the heart business. He wants His people to share the inward likeness of his Son. He wants us to achieve a heart that bears resemblance to the heart of the Son, who is like the Father in every way. He is not interested in self-imposed routines, Christian-based or otherwise, that make us *appear* Christ-like. He wants us to *be* Christ-like.

Even knowing that, however, I still struggled to figure out how to help these men make that kind of heart change. After six months of sharing with them every Christian doctrine I thought applied to their situation, I had exhausted my understanding. Many of the men in our ministry looked as if they had turned their lives around and were ready to go out into the world as new people, to live a life free of addiction, and to make a difference for God in a new way. Most were very thankful to God for all that had been done for them, and some were even ready to seek opportunities in full-time ministry. But their continued struggles and failures after they left the program indicated that something remained broken.

The "Discovery" of Transformation

I remember sitting at my desk begging God to tell me what to do next. My need was intense because I was losing people I loved. I had tried everything I had learned from experience and from church teachings, but nothing produced lasting results. These men had accomplished a noteworthy behavior change, but clearly their hearts had not been altered as much as their behavior.

"What do I say to the guys?" was the cry of my heart as Beth and I realized how discouraged we were about these men. We deeply felt the Lord's love for them, and had a great deal of hope for them, but many continued to fall back into their old patterns. So I put it to God in this statement of where I stood: "I have got to bring these men a message that works, or I have to bail."

As I mentioned earlier, God answered my prayer. It came as a single strong impression that played out in my mind as a conversation. To summarize the experience, it came down to a question and an answer.

Why don't you still weigh nearly 300 pounds like you used to?

Because you have been rewired. That is not who you are now. You are actually a different person.

I realized then that being a "different person" meant having a different heart. I thought about how different I am from those days. My life before becoming a Christian was one of heartbreak, misery, depression, and pain. It drove me to all kinds of self-destructive behavior, pursued in the interest of overpowering those feelings or separating myself from them. The list included gluttony, promiscuity, alcohol abuse, driving my car wildly, and on and on and on. As I contemplated the changes in my life, the voice in my head continued:

Your heart has been rewired, and you have become a different person. And that person has a whole new life that goes with the new heart.

I immediately remembered how important it was for me to leave the town of my old life and move on to a new one, which I did soon after my conversion. The answer to my prayer then was this: In order to truly be free of a behavior that is destroying our quality of life, we have to become someone to whom that behavior no longer appeals. That means the old person must die and a new person must be born.

I like the way Paul expresses this idea in his letter to the Colossians:

> *Do not lie to one another, seeing that you have stripped off the old self with its practices and have clothed yourselves with the new [spiritual self], which is [ever in the process of being] renewed and remolded into [fuller and more perfect knowledge upon] knowledge after the image (the likeness) of Him Who created it.*
>
> Colossians 3:9

I vividly remember the immediate freedom I received at conversion. The urge to go drinking several nights a week was no longer within me. I did nothing to achieve that. The desire simply vanished. So my conversion did bring with it some immediate healing and a new nature that desires good.

But I also can look back on my life and see that I still had many self-destructive behaviors to deal with after becoming a Christian. Even now, there are things I need to address in my ongoing transformation, and I know the challenges will continue until I go to be with Christ.

Fix Me

Once I had embraced the truth that the transformed heart is the only true way to be free, the next question arose: Why does our approach to change ourselves so often fail?

The answer unfolded as I looked honestly at my perspective when I began tackling my own undesirable behaviors. I did not want to suffer the consequences of my behavior, but I also didn't want to do any work or give up any of my errant values or beliefs. I just wanted to be fixed! I paid my counselor good money, and I expected her to do the work. In my mind, it was a straightforward exchange: Pay your money, get your healing.

The desire to "get fixed" is typical in our culture. We want to avoid the painful results of our actions, but don't want to change how we live our lives. In my case, I didn't want to give up "pain medicine" in the forms of food, alcohol, titillating media, etc. Upon identifying that thought process in me, I began to see it in my contemporaries and in the guys in our ministry. They wanted to be free of the suffering that the addiction had caused, period. There was no deep thought applied to what it takes to become a person who is not addicted. This attitude is not only typical with addictions, but with any behavior that is not easy for us to resist. Any behavior we cannot control is a form of bondage that causes us suffering, regardless of its social acceptability or legality.

Our "Quick Fix" Culture

In our culture, everybody is seeking a quick fix. Our approach to weight loss is a good example of this. And it's a subject with which I am all too familiar. Just consider what typically happens after most people complete a weight loss program. They eventually gain all or more of the weight back. This is certainly what happened to me. Everyone seems to understand this, but we cling to the expectation or delusion that the next fad diet will do the trick. The truth is that the next fad diet or any diet will not provide the long-term solution unless it is preceded by a commitment to a God-centered change of heart.

Being overweight to the point of obesity was a central theme of my life through my 30s. My struggle is familiar to most people who are overweight and take action to slim down. Over the course of five or six formal diet plans, plus untold informal ones, I lost and regained several hundred pounds. My parents even put me in the care of experts at a fat camp one summer. I had great short-term results, but I put the weight back on within about three months of returning home. The camp counselors knew how to help me lose weight, but they did not know how to help me address the heart causes of my obesity.

Throughout my dieting years, I never understood that I needed to change who I was. I just wanted to be thin. I tried dozens of deadend diets, but never had an enduring weight loss. Of course it wasn't the diets that were the problem. As expected, every diet that resulted in me burning more calories than I ate was successful. My particular dead-end came from the fact that my heart was still committed to being comforted or distracted by eating.

In every diet, I was trying to deal with the *consequences* rather than the *causes* of overeating. Never once did I expect to continue eating at a reduced level that would sustain the new lower weight. In fact, I motivated myself to stick to my diet with the anticipation of what I planned to eat at the end of the deprivation death march. From day one, I looked forward to a return to my old ways immediately upon hitting the magic number on the scale.

I was a victim of the false belief perpetuated in our culture that there is a quick fix for everything. The lie is that we can end the consequences of our heart's condition without addressing why our heart drives us to make bad choices. We are not looking for a heart change; we just want the problem to go away with the least possible inconvenience.

I have seen this lie at work in my own life and in the lives of others who seek freedom from their problems. It is in our nature to look for a quick, superficial solution to our problem, whether it's a trip to the doctor for a pill, or a new routine, religious or otherwise, that will facilitate the change. Sometimes our short-cut solutions involve transferring our problems to someone else. An example would be a woman who convinces herself that getting a divorce and marrying someone else will fix her discontent with life. The problem is that unless she has done something to change her heart, the discontent is likely to return after the excitement of a new relationship wears off. Divorce statistics indicate that second marriages have a higher probability of failing than first marriages. Those statistics would be very different if compliance with God's laws always came before taking an action under divorce law.

Transformation Means Heart and Life Change

As I began to construct a message for my brothers in the program that night, I became more convinced that transformation was not only the message for that time, but it was the core message for all Christians for all time. As it says in Romans 12, we are called to be transformed. The Scripture also says that we are to die to self and become new in Christ. It was my place to put that truth into words that would sink in, to plant seeds that could be watered and then watch the Lord bring life.

I wondered what it would take to become a new person and what it meant to have a new life in Christ. What would a new life look like? To answer that question, I took a cursory look at what had changed in my life.

These days I avoid movies, television shows, books and magazines that contain sex, violence, or profanity. I no longer go to bars or reminisce about my old life. I knew those activities would not only medicate my negative feelings, but had the power to lure me into more bad behavior. They represented the haunts of my old heart, which was the core of a life that wasn't worth living. I don't want that old life, that old heart, or that old person, so I don't want to expose myself to those influences. I am both repulsed by my old habits and wary of their potential influence. If you had accompanied me on the first 22 years of my transformation process, you would have observed those activities slowly disappearing from my life, and you would appreciate the stark contrast between the life I led then and the one I enjoy now and am determined to protect.

Paul had it right when he asked the Corinthians:

For what partnership have right living and right standing with God with iniquity and lawlessness? Or how can light have fellowship with darkness?

2 Corinthians 6:14

The clearly implied answer, of course, is that you cannot be in right standing with God if you are living a life filled with darkness. The changes in my life may seem small, but they added up to radical transformation. Some changes were required for transformation, while others seemed to arise from my transformation.

Let me explain. If someone wants to be free of his drug addiction, one of the first things he has to give up is going back to his old haunts where his dealer hangs out. It's hard to deny that hanging around people who promote drug use makes it virtually impossible to stay drug-free. If an addict likes his pusher and insists on having a relationship with him, the chances are less than slim that he will remain straight. Many times when men in our ministry program relapse, it is because they return to the old neighborhood. So that is a behavior change that is *required* for transformation.

In contrast, a behavior change that *results* from transformation occurs when drug users become repulsed by drugs and the drug culture and are unwilling to do anything that exposes them to that world. They might end relationships, change careers, or move if that is what it takes to succeed in their new life. And that is the kind of change I knew God wanted for the guys we were seeking to help.

Transformation Changes Our Life Perspective

Now let's look at the results of transformation. Take the example of a man who is an avid sports fan. Let's say it is monumentally important to him for his team to win. The outcome of the game affects his sense of well-being, his self-esteem, and his quality of life. If that man were transformed, he would realize that his self-worth comes from a relationship with Christ, the source of perfect love and grace. He would begin to see how silly his sports obsession was and lose interest in it, because his sense of well-being would no longer depend on his team's performance.

In the heart of the untransformed man who has indistinguishably enmeshed his sense of well-being with the success of his team, the team's losses can produce a negative response that he feels driven to escape from by engaging in self-destructive behaviors. The more intense the negative feeling, the more intense the separating behavior must be to overcome it.

To consider how that might unfold differently in a transformed life, consider my experiences. On becoming a Christian, I really had no idea what to expect. By the time I was ready to hear what Christianity was about, the only thing I understood was that the epicenter of all truth seemed to dwell in the Bible. One of my father's values, knowing the truth, kicked in, so I began a journey to understand it. This search led to the surprising realization that my life needed radical transformation to become one worth living.

My Christian self-help approach began with the diligent pursuit of techniques, processes, or new understandings that would eliminate the consequences of bad behaviors perfected during the first 26 years of my life. I sought out the latest, faddish solution that promised a breakthrough. Some of it was temporarily helpful.

Most of the things I pursued were quick-fix approaches. I really had no comprehension of what I had to give up. Had I known in advance what it would take to pursue the Christian life with integrity, I might have committed my life to Christ much later, or not at all. My life without Christ would have continued, characterized by pursuing further degenerate behaviors prompted by my belief that life was a miserable curse interspersed with moments of carnal distraction.

It is really hard for us to look forward to killing off our old, failed life, even in the depths of our misery. Most of us don't even hope for a new life, but vaguely envision a pain-free one that mysteriously starts working. So the conscious pursuit of a new life to end the pain of the old doesn't seem realistic, and that is exactly what Satan wants you to believe. However, Christ promises you something else: A new life in Him.

The thriving, self-help world may promise that disciplines such as positive self-talk or dietary routines are effective in bringing life-long change. But experience proves otherwise. Although these tactics may work for some for a time, they fail miserably and immediately for most others.

Transformation is a Heart Level Change That Drives a New Exterior

True life change requires transformation, and that is something that only occurs in the heart. Much of the self-help world is focused on developing a new routine or an understanding of what makes us tick. But its gurus rarely call us to address the core places in the heart that drive who we are and how we behave. Psychotherapy and religion, as they are often practiced, focus on establishing layer after oppressive layer of routine or belief. These layers can change the way we look and act on the outside, but they do little to affect true change at the core of who we are.

Alcoholics Anonymous is a great example. While some have experienced heart-level change through AA, most who maintain sobriety have not achieved freedom from their addiction. In fact, they often feel such freedom is unattainable. Success for AA participants can amount to wrapping their addiction in a new routine of beliefs and practices that prevent them from drinking. Yet, the torment of the addiction is ever present.

I know without asking that God is not satisfied with sobriety that allows the underlying bondage of addiction to continue. Didn't Jesus come to set the captives free, truly free on a heart level? He tells us He did by quoting Isaiah's prophecy about Himself:

> *The Spirit of the Lord [is] upon Me, because He has anointed Me [the Anointed One, the Messiah] to preach the good news (the Gospel) to the poor; He has sent Me to announce release to the captives and recovery of sight to the blind, to send forth as delivered those who are oppressed [who are downtrodden, bruised, crushed, and broken down by calamity], To proclaim the accepted and acceptable year of the Lord [the day when salvation and the free favors of God profusely abound.]*
>
> Luke 4:18-19

White-knuckled "Freedom"

There is no freedom from temptation without transformation. Pick your church, your self-help authority, your psychotherapy, your whatever. None of them can provide the liberty you're seeking without transformation.

Any proposition that offers freedom from self-destructive behavior by replacing it with something else isn't freedom. It is substitution. And substitution does not eliminate the torment of addiction. Ask yourself honestly if attending AA meetings for 20 years to maintain sobriety is freedom. While it may facilitate sobriety, many AA regulars have admitted to me that they are barely hanging on, and without regular attendance, they couldn't stay sober. That tells me that person is still laboring in bondage. In these discussions, I often hear the groans of a heart that desires to be free of temptation and of the white-knuckled struggle to stay sober one day at a time.

Further proof that the addiction is not conquered is evident among substance abusers who switch addictions. I know a person who replaced alcohol consumption with gluttony. He still had to attend AA meeting religiously to keep from drinking. Obviously addiction was still an issue. Is the answer to now attend Overeaters Anonymous or to mend the common thread of addiction – the heart?

And so it goes. Addicts adopt an outer veneer of socially acceptable behavior, but on the inside they are still subjected to a death march of constant heart-driven temptation. That is why the dieter puts the weight back on . . . why the guys in the program go back to drugs after seven months of being steeped in the Word . . . why AA participants fall off the wagon after years of sobriety or stay on the wagon but live a life in bondage to a new master.

The Transformation Message Challenges Our Behaviors

It is tempting to avoid the message of transformation because it means our current selves have to be denied. They must be starved out of existence. Committing to transformation means making unpleasant decisions. It means having to challenge behaviors that our heart desires. It means saying "no" to gossip or gluttony, drunkenness or drug abuse, child abuse or rage, violent films or pornography. Whatever negative acts that we engage in and don't want to give up must go. It is message of denial, of starvation, and of suffocation that few want to think about, counsel about, hear preached about, or show leadership in.

As Peter wrote to the early Christians, who struggled with their own sin natures:

Beloved, I implore you as aliens and strangers and exiles [in this world] to abstain from the sensual urges (the evil desires, the passions of the flesh, your lower nature) that wage war against the soul

1 Peter 2:11

A Transformed Heart Will Lose Interest in Ungodliness

The good news about transformation is that when you allow your heart to be changed, the pull of those formerly precious behaviors weakens, and eventually they become no more alluring than any other behavior you choose not to pursue. As the heart changes, the life changes as a natural result. The desires change, the decisions change, and the associated quality of life changes. The people you enjoy being around will change. Old friends may be left behind if they are not on a similar journey. Your church may change, your career may change. Not because they will be pried out of your desperate white-knuckled hand by some counselor or discipline, but because your transformed heart's desire will lead you to make different choices.

Just as my heart once led me to get drunk four nights a week, it now leads me to what it currently desires, and it literally never desires to get drunk. To affect the change we want, we must pursue transformation in the heart, confident that what now seems impossible to give up will actually lose its hold on your heart. Old habits will lose their appeal. Over time, your old self and your old ways will require effort even to remember.

Focus on the fact that the transformation process is

one designed by and rooted in God's perfect love for us. He would not taunt us with freedom and then make it unattainable. In fact, He will implement change in every heart made available to Him. Our job is to align ourselves with His spiritual laws, and as we do, transformation will occur.

Supporting Scripture References:

1. "Therefore be imitators of God [copy Him and follow His example], as well-beloved children [imitate their father]." Ephesians 5:1.

"For once you were darkness, but now you are light in the Lord; walk as children of Light [lead the lives of those native-born to the Light]." Ephesians 5:8

2. "For You did form my inward parts; You did knit me together in my mother's womb. I will confess and praise You for You are fearful and wonderful and for the awful wonder of my birth! Wonderful are Your works, and that my inner self knows right well." Psalm 139:13-14

3. "By means of these He has bestowed on us His precious and exceedingly great promises, so that through them you may escape [by flight] from the moral decay (rottenness and corruption) that is in the world because of covetousness (lust and greed), and become sharers (partakers) of the divine nature." 2 Peter 1:4

4. "[The Father] has delivered and drawn us to Himself out of the control and the dominion of darkness and has transferred us into the kingdom of the Son of His love," Colossians 1:13

5. "In Him you also who have heard the Word of Truth, the glad tidings (Gospel) of your salvation, and have believed in and adhered to and relied on Him, were stamped with the seal of the long-promised Holy Spirit. That [Spirit] is the guarantee of our inheritance [the first fruits, the pledge and foretaste, the down payment on our heritage], in anticipation of its full redemption and our acquiring [complete] possession of it—to the praise of His

glory."   Ephesians 1:13-14
"... The Spirit Whom He has caused to dwell in us ..."
                                              James 4:5

6. "For now we are looking in a mirror that gives only a
dim (blurred) reflection [of reality as in a riddle or enigma],
but then [when perfection comes] we shall see in reality and
face to face! Now I know in part (imperfectly), but then I
shall know and understand fully and clearly, even in the
same manner as I have been fully and clearly known and
understood [by God]."   1 Corinthians 13:12

7. "Such [practices] have indeed the outward appearance
[that popularly passes] for wisdom, in promoting self-
imposed rigor of devotion and delight in self-humiliation
and severity of discipline of the body, but they are of no
value in checking the indulgence of the flesh (the lower
nature). [Instead, they do not honor God but serve only to
indulge the flesh.]"   Colossians 2:23

Chapter Five

Semper Fidelis
(Always Faithful)

*Be transformed (changed) by the [entire] re-
newal of your mind [by its new ideals and its
new attitude].*

Romans 12:2

One of the greatest shocks of my Christian walk occurred five years after my conversion when the realization
struck that I was miserable . . . again. It was unexpected
and seemed unlikely given the dramatic change in direction
my life had taken since the moment of conversion. I had
gone from a life that in many ways resembled a curse that
no dog should have to endure to a new life based upon the
ultimate truth. So why did I find myself back at a point of
despair after experiencing that "new Christian" glow?

Displaying all the usual "baby Christian" symptoms,
I was ready to talk openly about my faith and was even
delusional enough to consider taking on teaching or preaching or maybe even becoming an elder! In all of my Christian
immaturity, I felt ready to be listened to about the myster-
ies of Christianity, a condition not uncommon to green,
"on-fire" believers.

While possibly qualified to talk about why I *became* a Christian, I was in no shape to talk about the transforming walk of *being* a Christian. I had just not done that part. I was caught up in a name-it-and-claim-it approach to Christianity, even though its promises were mysteriously absent from my life. After five years, I was depressed, dejected, and needing answers to the mystery of my spiritual derailment. [1]

Using symptoms to diagnose the cause, I could only conclude that the change in my life had been superficial. All the wounds, sins, and junk of my pre-Christian days were still driving my heart. Since my Christian fervor had waned over time, there was nothing to distract me or remove me from experiencing the full effect of a heart, which, although committed to God, was essentially untransformed.

In that state, I was no longer able to substitute my fresh Christian excitement about the *promise* of an abundant life for the *reality* of an abundant life. That life was not available given the condition of my heart. My new Christian zeal had in essence become the medication I now relied on to separate me from whatever I didn't want to feel. Just like the person who thinks that getting married is going to improve his or her entire life, I thought that Christianity was going to straighten out my life, providing an easy fix.

Well, I was partly right. God's Truth in its entirety was the answer, but I was living my *decision* instead of my *religion*. I was proceeding under the assumption that the hard part was committing my life to Christ, and that all His promises would automatically follow. Changing my life to conform to His laws was not on my agenda. In essence, I had an unspoken contract with God that if I committed my life to Christ, He would commit to fix what was wrong with me. I had made the decision; it was up to Him to do the work.

For a while, I even thought it was working. I fooled my heart with a concoction of new Christian excitement combined with name-it-and-claim-it expectations. However, I was still carrying a lot of baggage into my relationship with Christ. Fortunately for me, He had the answer for my condition. It was centered on *responding* to God's call to be transformed into His image, to share in His divine nature, and to inwardly resemble the heart of His Son. I would never enjoy the rich Christ-centered life I wanted by resting on my conversion experience. Bottom line: Conversion made me eligible to receive God's promises and improve my quality of life, but it did not give me the transformed heart needed to usher in that new life.

In other words, at the moment of conversion, we are deemed righteous through faith in the Son and are promised a rewarding Christian life. But to claim that new life, our hearts must conform to His laws.

We are to work diligently at becoming vessels that are not only able to house God and Christ through the Holy Spirit, but that will carry out God's perfect plan for our lives. The time has come to seek the fully abundant life by pursuing God and being open to His transformation. Is that not the course you want to be on?

Motivated by both despair and a desire to know the truth, I unknowingly set out on a 24-year process of transformation that continues today. It is ongoing, because if we are supposed to be transformed into the image of Christ to the point of resembling Him, then I will still be on this journey when my "earth suit" checks out. [2]

One of my early revelations after committing my life to Christ occurred when I realized that the promises of the Christian life, which I was so ready to have heaped upon me, were not available by Christ's singular redemptive act that conveyed me into the Kingdom. While I did receive some instant relief in my dysfunctional and painful life, I was not striding swiftly and powerfully with a sure-footed Christian walk. I was a man who had received forgiveness from my Lord but was still loaded down with emotional,

behavioral and heart wounds. I needed to submit and
conform my heart to the laws of God in order to dwell in
the peace and joy that are promised to believers. It was
time to unload the junk I had brought into my relationship
with God.

I was encouraged in my journey by these words
from Romans:

> *For those whom He foreknew [of whom He was aware and
> knew beforehand], He also destined from the beginning [fore-
> ordaining them] to be molded into the image of His Son
> [and share inwardly His likeness], that He might become
> the firstborn among many brethren.*
>
> Romans 8:29

Opening the Heart to Change

Virtually every man Beth and I worked with at the
drug rehab program shared the condition that dominated
my early Christian years. Even those counselees who were
long-time believers or pastors lacked the heart-level transformation that was needed to confront the source of their
self-defeating behavior.

In trying to demonstrate to the guys in the program
what I meant by transformation, how it occurs, and what is
required to get results, the U.S. Marine Corps came to mind
as a fitting analogy. I once had the good fortune of having a
business partner who is a retired Marine. From him, I
quickly found out that you do not work for the Marines,
you *become* a Marine, and you remain a Marine even after
you retire or leave the Corps. As we discussed his military
experiences, I could easily see that the internal transformation from a recruit into a Marine was strikingly similar to
the heart transformation that was so desperately needed by
the men in the program.

Imagine the young man or woman who has considered everything central to and appealing about the Marines finally deciding to take the noble plunge of becoming one. They have read through all the recruiting material, while pondering how accomplished they will feel as a Marine. They understand and may well expect to be changed into something other than what they are today. So on an intellectual level at least, they desire to change their lives. But somewhere inside them is the deeper desire to not only act like a Marine, but to have the heart of a Marine.

It is having the heart of a Marine that makes you one. Recruits know that involves inner change. The values and ideals at the heart of the institution and in the hearts of the Marines themselves are presented and reinforced in all the marketing materials, perhaps most succinctly communicated by the Marine motto: *"Semper Fidelis."* Usually spoken as a resolute heart burst – *"SEMPER FI!"* – it means "always faithful." Faithful to God, to country, and to fellow Marines.

Decision made, the new recruits sign up and report for duty, having made a commitment to conform to the values and requirements of being a Marine. As inductees, all the trappings of their lives change as they are immediately put through boot camp. They begin to get up really early, train really hard, and learn to deal with a particularly pesky and exacting sergeant, who feels that loud, direct, and nose-touching closeness is the most effective way to communicate. The daily routines alone are life-changing. Forced marches, tough physical conditioning, and all the rest of the demands of this new, rigorous life test their determination and their ability to persevere. They are challenged to live the new values they have committed to uphold.

Surrounding them in everything they do and hear, the values of being a Marine begin to soak in. At first, the outward activities and Marine-like behavior feel unnatural and forced. Who they are in the first days bears little resemblance to what they are striving to become. But the soaking in continues through the first layer of their outward behavior and goes progressively deeper. This soaking in occurs because of their decision to allow it.

The recruit's mind and body respond to the new values and new rigors with a growing sense of acceptance and routine. Although painfully slow at first, the transformation from within has begun. New skills, values, and attitudes replace urges to rebel and quell any lingering doubts about their decision to enlist. Being a Marine becomes who they are, not only in their career, but in their hearts. It best describes the core of who they are as people.

When the training is over, they are ready to be pronounced Marines. The official graduation and certification of the recruits as active Marines is recognition that they have successfully completed all their requirements. But what *really* makes them Marines is what has happened on the inside. They have accepted the values of the Marines into their hearts and discarded their old, conflicting traits. The Marines we see on the outside reflect who they are on the inside. There is no conflict between their hearts and their exteriors. The freshly minted Marines bear little resemblance to the recruits who joined the Corps some months before.

After Marines have served, they return to civilian life as very different people, with very different hearts. How differently will they now make decisions about life and lifestyle? How differently will they act as a father or mother, a husband or wife, a friend? How differently will they decide about career and life purpose? And how differently will they regard their country? They have been transformed into new beings from the heart side out. They are truly different people, suffering few conflicts between their hearts and their exteriors.

The exact point at which transformation occurs in the recruit's heart is far more difficult to determine than

understanding the process that drives it. While it was not
the decision to become a Marine that results in the transformation, there can be no change without it. And if the
decision to become a Marine is made without the willingness to become a new creation on a heart level, then the
transformation will never occur either. [3]

Transformation occurs because the recruits allow
themselves to be changed. It is not because they work hard.
No amount of boot camp or forced external activity will
change a heart that is closed to change. Recruits must make
a conscious decision to open their hearts to the ideals and
attitudes of the Marine Corps. For many recruits, the
hardest "work" is mustering up the humility required for
the process. Fortunately, as personal imperfections are
revealed and embraced, humility follows. And that humility
enables them to complete the selfless and sacrificial act of
dying to themselves in order to become a Marine. The final
destination of transformation is the place where being a
Marine and acting like a Marine are the same, void of any
internal conflicts. It is a place where the skin fits, and they
no longer need to suppress the desires of their hearts in
order to be the people they want to be. [4]

What we have more commonly in our world are
people whose public exteriors bear little resemblance to
their hearts' motivations. We can observe this in a variety
of situations, ranging from the person who struggles not to
shop obsessively to the sober alcoholic who wages a daily
war of sobriety with his heart. Each of these situations
starts with the decision to be free of the self-destructive
behavior, but does not result in victory or in freedom from
the temptation.[5]

Is a person free who successfully keeps from drinking for 30 years but depends on weekly AA meetings to stay
sober? Have they been transformed at a heart level, or are
they simply able to muster the drive to stay sober against
their continuous desire to drink? Achieving sobriety is a

critical piece of solving the puzzle, and we should all be thankful that the AA organization exists. Without sobriety you cannot get to the next level of healing and transformation. But what about true freedom? Certainly, every person on the planet who has sought to change themselves for the better desires to be truly free of the underlying struggle, not just the undesirable behavior.

As Christians, we also should strive to reach that place where our exterior reflects our heart's motivation. However, what we do more often is go to a new church, buy the latest self-help book, join a support group, or enter into a new relationship to help us fix whatever we deem to be wrong with our lives. Few of us approach our desire to change like new Marine recruits do, with the understanding that we will have to become a new person from the heart side out.

Instead, we try to *act* like a new person with the help of some belief or technique. But that is just applying veneer. The veneer will work for some amount of time, maybe even a long time. At some point, though, it will wear off from the inside out because the true inner person will chafe against the poorly fitting exterior. Or, some life event will wear through the external veneer to the heart, causing a return to the old behavior. Freedom from a behavior we struggle against does not come from acting like we are free. We need to *become* that free person. We need to allow our hearts to be transformed and put to death the habits and routines that supported the old person. [6]

Compare the Marine recruit's experience to that of someone who has decided that it is time to finally take off some unwanted weight. I doubt the new recruit fully understands the magnitude of their commitment or anticipates the profoundly different person that awaits them at their discharge. But few have missed the point that they are to become someone new. In contrast, the dieter's only interest is in losing weight; he or she has no desire to *truly* deal with the heart level cause of overeating. He fully expects to temporarily deny himself an activity that is as much a part of who he is as his preference in music. Instead of desiring to become the kind of person who naturally weighs 20 pounds less, a dieter intends to fight the temptations and desires of who they are long enough to drop the weight. Many dieters are successful at hitting their weight loss target. The heart problem is obvious as many actually motivate themselves to lose weight with the promise that they will be able to eat more when it is all over. There is no heart change there.

The old desire to eat at a level beyond need will continue to rage. If anything, the dieter's strategy of temporary self-denial actually fuels the drive to overeat as a reward for his or her sacrifice. As a result, most dieters, including myself, regain their weight, sometimes even exceeding their previous weight. Trying to become a person who naturally stays thinner simply by dieting is as much a deadend strategy as trying to cure skin cancer by applying makeup.

Recruits who decide to become Marines succeed at a far greater rate than dieters become and remain thinner. It is all about the heart. The Marine recruits commit to a world that develops them into different people. They have committed their hearts to becoming someone new, and they open their hearts to change. That change is first fueled by their commitment to the goal which they seek. Then, it is driven by the willingness to endure the necessary discomfort of denying the old self so that the new self can emerge and be established.

Fortunately for Christians, our greatest challenge is to decide to allow our hearts to be changed by the new ideas and attitudes that come from the new nature we receive through faith in Christ. Our hardest work is embracing the truth about the condition of our heart and conforming to God's laws. It is powerful encouragement that Jesus says His yoke is light. As Christians, we have the option to pursue the veneer of a desirable lifestyle or pursue transformation. Scripture tells us that we can achieve inner peace and abundant life when we substitute His life-giving laws for the bonds of worldly lies.

The Lord does not want us to simply apply a veneer of piety that rages against our hearts. Neither is it His plan for us to suffer a life of temptation that defeats and discourages us. God does not just want recovering substance abusers to build a routine of sobriety around His name. Instead, He desires a new, transformed life for us, a life free of bondage from the irresistible temptations that drive self-destructive behavior.

Count on temptation to always be present, but as we are transformed, we are able to resist it in stride. That is the promise of God. It is up to us to decide that we will do whatever it takes to become new in Him. Our decision to pursue God's heart transformation process, combined with His promise to see it through to the end, is a formula for assured success. For He is *Semper Fidelis* ... Always Faithful.

Supporting Scripture References:

1. "Therefore, you will fully know them by their fruits."
Matthew 7:20

2. "... so that you may prove [for yourselves] what is the good and acceptable will of God, even the things which are good and acceptable and perfect [in His sight for you].
Romans 12:2

3. "... be transformed (changed) by the [entire] renewal of your mind [by its new ideals and its new attitude]..."
Romans 12:2

4. "And put on the new nature (the regenerate self) created in God's image, [Godlike] in true righteousness and holiness."
Ephesians 4:24

5. "Strip yourselves of your former nature [put off and discard your old unrenewed self] which characterized your previous manner of life and becomes corrupt through lusts and desires that spring from delusion."
Ephesians 4:22

6. "For those whom He foreknew [of whom He was aware and loved beforehand], He also destined from the beginning [foreordaining them] to be molded into the image of His Son [and share inwardly His likeness], that He might become the firstborn among many brethren."
Romans 8:29

Chapter Six

A House Divided

You [are like] unfaithful wives [having illicit love affairs with the world and breaking your marriage vow to God]! Do you not know that being the world's friend is being God's enemy? So whoever chooses to be a friend of the world takes his stand as an enemy of God.

James 4:4

And if a house is divided (split into factions and rebelling) against itself, that house will not be able to last.

Mark 3:25

The first graduation Beth and I attended for men in the rehab program was a powerful experience. Held in the chapel, the graduates of the residential addiction recovery program occupied the front row. Making the best of donated clothes, they were looking good! All of their faces were beaming with joy and excitement. From their perspective, they had not only survived the challenges of rehab, but were celebrating a great life victory.

My eyes scanned the row of men prepared to graduate, looking for each man Beth and I had worked with during the previous months. Not all of the men who had started with the group were in attendance. Some had given up and gone back to their old lives, believing things would be different this time. They weren't. We had experienced the heartbreak of working with one man who bailed out by leaving the program unannounced during the night. Another man was kicked out for breaking a key rule in the last week before graduation. So we were glad to see each of our remaining guys in the front row, looking proud of what he had accomplished.

These men were not in this program because they had been caught driving drunk or had shown up for work with alcohol on their breath. Most had been through other recovery programs, but had failed to maintain sobriety during or after each one. Some had been actively abusing substances for most of their lives. Some had held jobs for brief periods, often just long enough to accumulate money to acquire their drug of choice. Many were here by court order. Most had been homeless at some point. Others had known only the street for majority of their lives. When these men entered the program, they had already lost at the game of life many times over. All of them were in tough shape when they arrived. They came there with their addiction at full throttle to join a program which was their only and possibly last hope.

But that was seven months ago for our glowing counselees. Today they appeared to be totally transformed. Their once empty, sunken eyes were now sparkling with hope and excitement. The anticipation of getting their lives back on track was bursting out of every pore. Today was a day of new beginnings. Most of them had already gotten jobs and found a church home. A few had even been reunited with estranged family members. Things were looking pretty good for these guys. Yes, they knew that there were still obstacles to overcome out in the real world, unprotected by a residence program, but they were convinced they would succeed. These men had come to depend on their faith, which had grown tremendously during the weeks of being steeped in the Word and ministered to by people they knew were working there to love and serve them.

The proceedings began with songs from their own choir. Soulful, rhythmic music lifted me and everybody in the room as we worshiped the God who truly is the only hope for any of us to have a life worth living. As the stirring praise songs lifted us all out of our chairs, my heart was overcome with joy and thanksgiving for the God who loves me and them, and who brought us here to experience His love for these men.

The sermon followed. It was a moving message that went straight to the point and was full of truth. The preacher was both joyful and solemn about the significance of this day, the truth of addiction, and the power God wields to free us from our suffering. It was a powerful message that was far too raw for most Sunday morning church services. Yet it spoke directly to my heart, moving me to wonder if my family could find a church with this much spiritual power to attend every Sunday.

Next, each graduate was called to the stage to receive his diploma and make a brief speech. The crowd's enthusiasm never subsided. In fact, the energy built as each man walked up three steps to the stage and looked over the crowd to the sound of raucous applause and cat calls. Many men choked back tears as they spoke of their love for God and gave Him all the credit for their changed lives. A few of them thanked family members in the audience, some of whom responded with impromptu speeches expressing deep gratitude for the recovery of a son, brother or husband. The crowd's applause broke forth at every opportunity, expressing gratitude and joy for all that unfolded.

There were 10 graduates that day. We left the ceremonies filled with a sense of well-being and a sort of completing joy. It made us grateful that we had been led to minister in this place. As we drove off, we knew that we had been part of something really powerful, and we felt a no-strings-attached gratitude for being used to advance God's Kingdom. Our hearts were full.

On the Monday after Friday's graduation, we called one of the program staff members and learned that three of the ten graduates had been caught using drugs or drinking the night of graduation and had been kicked out of the after-care program. Over the next several days, we got reports that several more of the men, who had proclaimed themselves free of addiction and had not relapsed during their seven months in the program, were using drugs again. The ultimate result of all that commitment, investment, crying, and praising was that all but one of those men returned to their old habits. Only one or two that we were aware of was ever able to achieve consistent sobriety and get his life back on track.

The initial news of the graduates' relapses shocked and saddened us. God had really put His love for these men on our hearts, and we were heartbroken by this outcome. After hearing the final tally of failures in that graduating class, I became despondent thinking about what had gone wrong. Were they all pretending to be free of addiction? Had none of them actually changed? Did all of us misinterpret God's promises for these men? How could so many have failed? The proclamations of freedom and the glory they had made to God were as real as anything I had ever witnessed.

Why then did they fail? Why had these men, whose lives had clearly been affected by this ministry, who had not used illicit drugs for over half a year, who accurately quoted Scripture with understanding, and who stood confidently at the graduation ceremony, proclaiming that their drugging days were behind them, chose to go out and get high or drunk on graduation night or soon after?

Many of these men were committed believers, who had gained much confidence by proclaiming Scriptures such as "Resist Satan and he must flee." They put their faith in that spiritual law, believing it would be effective in keeping them drug free. They were as sure of their ability to resist evil as they were sure that if they released a Bible into thin air it would drop to the ground. After all, aren't God's spiritual laws as valid as his physical laws, like the law of gravity? And aren't all of them continually in force? Of course they are.

However, in ministering to other Christians for more than twenty years, I have seen many believers fail repeatedly to resist the temptation of a particular self-destructive behavior that they wanted to stop. As a new Christian, I had simply accepted that I had the authority to resist evil without condition since I had made a commitment to follow Christ. I never understood why I and others, including the men in the program, couldn't make this authority consistently work for us.

Why couldn't these men simply invoke that promise, be free of their addiction and get on with their lives? After all, Jesus was able to take on Satan, fight back three temptations that were tremendous by any standard, and then leave Satan with no victory. Aren't we supposed to share in the divine nature of Christ as His brothers and sisters? Haven't we been conveyed into God's Kingdom with power, authority and royalty? So what gives? Why can't we successfully and repeatedly resist the Devil on every temptation challenge of our lives?

Many Christians have done battle against temptation with that scriptural promise in their hearts, yet failed. Is it that the Scripture is not true, or is it somehow misinterpreted? The answer is that the promise is real and true, but *it is not the only truth in Scripture*, and it can't stand alone outside the context of other principles in the Bible. Gravity is not the only physical law either. If you hold the Bible in your hand with a force that equally opposes the force of gravity, the Bible will not fall. And if you apply more force than gravity, the Bible will rise. In the same way, we can not claim selected powers afforded us as Christians and ignore the rest, any more than you would attempt to walk on water, unless your life very closely emulated Christ's.

In the same Bible that instructs us to resist Satan so that he will flee, there are many other relevant Scriptures that we must consider. Let's look at two of them.

First, remember what Paul tells us in his letter to Ephesians, "Don't let the sun go down on your anger; do not allow Satan to gain a foothold."

Second, consider the parable in the book of Matthew about the unmerciful servant. In the parable, the king's servant was forgiven by the king of a great debt, but the king's servant was unwilling to forgive his servant for a far lesser debt. As punishment, the king turns over the unmerciful servant to the torturer. In the concluding words, Jesus warns that God will do the same to us if we do not forgive.

Both of these scriptures express spiritual laws regarding authority and Satan. In the first reference we are told that we have authority to resist Satan's temptations and avoid the consequences of giving in to him. In the second reference we are told that withholding forgiveness will give Satan access to torment us. Jesus concludes the unmerciful servant parable with the warning that God will turn us over to Satan if we do not forgive. It's a foreboding promise of something God is definitely going to do.

Some might wish that all this torment was to be the plight of nonbelievers and that these warnings were spelled out to motivate people to give their lives to Jesus. However, notice that this torment is not a consequence of rejecting salvation. In fact, both of these Scriptures are addressed to followers of Christ and describe the Kingdom of God. So it is those who have given their lives to Christ

who are being warned about unforgiveness and its consequences. We have the power and authority to resist Satan.
Or, if we choose to, we can give him the authority to
torment us. Christians are in control here. When we decide
not to forgive, we are in effect granting Satan permission to
torment us.

What's more, we cannot expect to be able to resist
Satan's temptations and torment if we have already given
him the authority to do so. Isn't that what we attempt to do
when we refuse to operate in forgiveness but still expect to
have the authority to make him flee? Unforgiveness brings
Satan glory and ushers his presence into our lives. We have
all heard about experiencing the presence of God. Well, we
also have the ability to experience the presence of Satan.
And as Christians, it is our choice. Unforgiveness is a
characteristic of Satan, and there is no trace of it or any sin
in Christ. In fact, Christ once said that there is was nothing
of Satan to be found in Him. The clear implication is that
He was victorious over Satan because there was no characteristic of Satan in Him. Since there is no unforgiveness or
sin in Christ, He was able to resist Satan. [1]

The same spiritual laws apply to us. If we are bringing glory to Satan through unforgiveness, in effect invoking
his presence, we cannot resist him. And God's promise is
that He will make sure Satan is informed of our sin and
dispatch him to torment us.[2]

For me and every man I worked with in the program, it was that torment in the form of emotional pain
that led us to suppress our intensely negative feelings with
some form of "medication." In the case of the guys, they
resorted to abusing intoxicants. As for me, I turned to a
whole host of worldly diversions, including drinking,
overeating, watching television and more. It was not until I
was able to forgive life-long offenses that I could begin to
control my self-destructive behaviors. Not until I was free
of the torment of bitterness and rage sustained by my

unforgiveness was I able to resist the harmful activities that separated me from those feelings.

Forgiveness does not come easy. Giving our lives to the Lord is not an act of forgiveness on our part. Rather, salvation is an act of forgiveness and grace on God's part. I was a Christian for more than five years before I confronted my need to forgive. During those years, I was in euphoric denial claiming all the truth that I felt applied to me as a brother of Christ. I operated on the belief that having given my life to Christ, the entire toolbox of God's promises and power was available for me to live a victorious life.

I am still amazed by how I was able to turn a deaf ear to Scriptures that required me to do something about the condition of my heart. The Bible's entire transformation message just went right over my head. It was not what I was looking for. I wasn't looking for a new heart. I was not looking for a way to break free of all of my medicating activities. I just wanted my crummy life fixed. I wanted to be that same person, but not to have to suffer the consequences of my behaviors.

It is really no surprise that after five years of such shallow Christianity, I felt nearly as bad as I had just before my conversion. I didn't realize that although being saved opened the door to heart transformation, I still had to walk through that door. Although my conversion was a miraculous act of God for which I was and still am deeply grateful, it did not transform me immediately into someone who was in compliance with all of God's spiritual laws. I had not done any of the heart-work needed to claim a new nature. I was still a vessel that grieved the Holy Spirit. As it says in the apostle John's first letter:

> By this it is made clear who take their nature from God and are His children and who take their nature from the devil and are his children: no one who does not practice righteous-

ness [who does not conform to God's will in purpose, thought, and action] is of God; neither is anyone who does not love his brother (his fellow believer in Christ).

1 John 3:10

Obeying God's Laws Frees Us from Torment

I found that the men in the drug rehab program were just like me and so many others who wanted to be free of something that is ruining their life or stealing their joy. They had checked in with the desire to be free, but almost none of them were ready to do the heart-work that true freedom required.

All of the truth was there – in their classes, counseling and study. But few were able to achieve heart-level change. Most were able to complete the program and not abuse any substance for seven months. They were doing fairly well physically and were in good shape mentally, but they still had that same heart that got them there in the first place. And that heart wanted to go back to their old ways, spend time with their same friends, watch the same movies, read the same books, sustain the same old resentments, and sleep with the same girl friend. Basically, they were sustaining Satan's presence in their lives, so that when it came time to resist substance abuse, they were powerless.

I have often thought what a significant opportunity it is for these men to take seven months out of their lives to focus on God's Word and be taught by people who love them. There is no wanting for the basics of life. A place to live, food to eat, some money to spend, and clothes to wear are all provided at no expense. They study the Word, eat, sleep, do job assignments, and pray every day. At my current rate of Bible reading and prayer, it would probably take me years to accomplish what they could do while taking a break from their lives for seven full months.

Of course, reading the Bible and praying is not the whole answer to accomplishing the life change they are after. It wasn't the answer for me in the early years of my faith, and it wasn't for our men in the program, or for anyone else who is closed to transformation. We absolutely do need to read and pray, but that's not enough. It is the difference between knowing and doing. Knowing the Word and praying to God doesn't mean that we share an inward likeness to Christ and share in His inheritance. Remember that we are told to build up our treasures in heaven. At salvation, there is no treasure chest awaiting us. We are called to build up those treasures.

Remember, Satan knows the Word and talks to God. His minions recognized Jesus on sight. He continually stands before God condemning every one of His children. There is no forgiveness in him. I'm thinking he probably doesn't have any treasures in heaven. The Word gives us specific direction about what we are to do and not do as Christians. In the process of obeying the wishes of God, we become more like Christ, act more like Christ, and therefore share in His inheritance, His abundant life, and His power. [3]

The Bible expresses this concept as follows:

But immorality (sexual vice) and all impurity [of lustful, rich, wasteful living] or greediness must not even be named among you, as is fitting and proper among saints (God's consecrated people). Let there be no filthiness (obscenity, indecency) nor foolish and sinful (silly and corrupt) talk, nor coarse jesting, which are not fitting or becoming; but instead voice your thankfulness [to God]. For be sure of this: that no person practicing sexual vice or impurity in thought or in life, or one who is covetous [who has lustful desire for the property of others and is greedy for gain]—for he [in effect] is an idolater—has any inheritance in the kingdom of Christ and of God.

Ephesians 5:3-5

We are also told not to grieve the Spirit. Obviously, we grieve the Spirit greatly by exhibiting the characteristics of Satan rather than honoring the wishes of God. If we are actively grieving the Spirit, what are the consequences? Will that help us experience the presence of God or transform us into the image of Christ? [4]

As for the graduates, I believe there were two basic causes of their failure. First, they had learned much about God's promises and Christian living, but they had accomplished little heart change. They had not come to put the old person within them to death; they were there to end their suffering. Second, they continued to behave in ways that grieved the Spirit by hosting the characteristics of Satan within a vessel that had been committed to God. We learned over time that the men who failed to stay drug-free were practicing behaviors that were clearly an affront to God and brought glory to Satan. I will not glorify Satan by listing his victories; all of them are specified in the Bible as things Christians are instructed not to do.

In life, there is no inheritance without a death. In the realm of our spiritual existence, that is also true. The old self must die. We must become a new being in Christ, aligning our actions with God's wishes for His children. That means we not only must know what to do, we must actually do it. The good news is that as we become obedient in small ways, we will grow in joy and strength to take on bigger challenges. However, we first must share His desire for our transformation. We cannot be satisfied with temporary exterior improvements; we must build a new foundation by pursuing transformation within. The exterior changes will naturally follow. If we are not seeking a new life, we will not have one. God wants us free from the torment, but all our flesh wants is to put an end to the consequences of a certain behavior.

> *We know that our old (unrenewed) self was nailed to the*
> *cross with Him in order that [our] body [which is the in-*
> *strument] of sin might be made ineffective and inactive for*
> *evil, that we might no longer be the slaves of sin.*
>
> Romans 6:6

This may be a shock to you, but God really is not in the business of freeing us from our torment. Actually, looking back on the parable of the unmerciful servant, God promises to deliver us to the tormentor. The apostle Paul in 1 Corinthians 5:5 also talks about handing errant members of the New Testament Church over to Satan to be tormented. Someone who pursues a relationship with God or who enters into a God-based recovery program just to get fixed will fail. People who want the quick-fix solution are looking for superficial answers that will end the torment, the suffering, and the consequences of who they are. They are unaware that they need to become someone new to be free of Satan's torment.

Some are quick to say that they can't believe in a God who would turn us over to Satan to be tormented, or that God would not relieve any suffering if we ask for His help. Yet, those beliefs ignore the fact that we are tormented because we break the laws of God. We are the ones who made the decision not to heed the laws of God, and therefore we are responsible for the torment. We always have the option of conforming to the law.

If we break the speed limit and get a ticket to pay as punishment, who is responsible for our punishment? The speeding law was put in place complete with consequences. It is totally up to us to abide by those laws if we want to avoid the consequences. Is the authority that put the speeding laws in place or the policeman that handed you the ticket being cruel, mean, or unkind? No. If you don't

like tickets, don't speed. You have to own the consequences.

The spiritual laws are put in place by God, and they
have consequences. So it makes no sense for us to petition
Him in prayer or in any other way to be relieved of what we
have brought upon ourselves. The way out is very clear.
Conform to the law. God actually wants us to love his laws.
Some would say that they can't. God's answer to that is to
be transformed to His image so that your heart will resemble the heart of Christ who loves His laws. God wants us to
conform to His law as any loving father wants the best for
his children.

God grants prayers that are consistent with His will
and His law. Freedom from bitterness, which is a torment
of unforgiveness, will not come from asking God to remove the bitterness. Nor will it come from a self-help
method that simply ends the destructive medicating behavior that dulls the feelings of bitterness. Freedom from
bitterness will come from a heart that has the humility to
forgive and that obeys the laws of God. [5]

One other closing thought. The police only catch a
small percentage of those who speed, but you cannot exist
outside of God's creation. The laws of God are built into
the foundation of the spiritual world. The spiritual world is
a 24/7 world. There is no time when His law doesn't apply
to you, and as a Christian you have allowed the Holy Spirit
(the mind of God) to take up residence within you.

How often would you speed if a policeman lived in
your back seat? More to the point, how many tickets would
you get if one appeared on your dashboard every time you
went one mile per hour over the speed limit?

God does not want your suffering. He wants your heart.
His laws make it so that you are never comfortable opposing His will for you.

When Christ, Who is our life, appears, then you also will

appear with Him in [the splendor of His] glory. So kill (deaden, deprive of power) the evil desire lurking in your members [those animal impulses and all that is earthly in you that is employed in sin]: sexual vice, impurity, sensual appetites, unholy desires, and all greed and covetousness, for that is idolatry (the deifying of self and other created things instead of God). It is on account of these [very sins] that the [holy] anger of God is ever coming upon the sons of disobedience (those who are obstinately opposed to the divine will), Among whom you also once walked, when you were living in and addicted to [such practices]. But now put away and rid yourselves [completely] of all these things: anger, rage, bad feeling toward others, curses and slander, and foulmouthed abuse and shameful utterances from your lips! Do not lie to one another, for you have stripped off the old (unregenerate) self with its evil practices.

Colossians 3:4-9

Supporting Scripture References:

1. "And you [He made alive], when you were dead (slain) by [your] trespasses and sins in which at one time you walked [habitually]. You were following the course and fashion of this world [were under the sway of the tendency of this present age], following the prince of the power of the air. [You were obedient to and under the control of] the [demon] spirit that still constantly works in the sons of disobedience [the careless, the rebellious, and the unbelieving, who go against the purposes of God]. Among these we as well as you once lived and conducted ourselves in the passions of our flesh [our behavior governed by our corrupt and sensual nature], obeying the impulses of the flesh and the thoughts of the mind [our cravings dictated by our senses and our dark imaginings]. We were then by nature children of [God's] wrath and heirs of [His] indignation, like the rest of mankind."   Ephesians 2:1-3

2. "And in wrath his master turned him over to the torturers (the jailers), till he should pay all that he owed. So also My heavenly Father will deal with every one of you if you do not freely forgive your brother from your heart his offenses."   Matthew 18:34-35

3. "So brace up your minds; be sober (circumspect, morally alert); set your hope wholly and unchangeably on the grace (divine favor) that is coming to you when Jesus Christ (the Messiah) is revealed. [Live] as children of obedience [to God]; do not conform yourselves to the evil desires [that governed you] in your former ignorance [when you did not know the requirements of the Gospel]. But as the One Who called you is holy, you yourselves also be holy in all your conduct and manner of living. For it is written, You shall be holy, for I am holy."   1 Peter 1:13-16

4. "And do not grieve the Holy Spirit of God [do not offend or vex or sadden Him], by Whom you were sealed (marked, branded as God's own, secured) for the day of redemption (of final deliverance through Christ from evil and the consequences of sin). Let all bitterness and indignation and wrath (passion, rage, bad temper) and resentment (anger, animosity) and quarreling (brawling, clamor, contention) and slander (evil-speaking, abusive or blasphemous language) be banished from you, with all malice (spite, ill will, or baseness of any kind). And become useful and helpful and kind to one another, tenderhearted (compassionate, understanding, loving-hearted), forgiving one another [readily and freely], as God in Christ forgave you."

Ephesians 4:30-32

5. "Delight yourself also in the Lord, and He will give you the desires and secret petitions of your heart."

Psalm 37:4

Chapter Seven

A Heart Restored

*The night is far gone and the day is almost here.
Let us then drop (fling away) the works and
deeds of darkness and put on the [full] armor of
light. Let us live and conduct ourselves honora-
bly and becomingly as in the [open light of]
day, not in reveling (carousing) and drunkenness, not in immorality and debauchery (sensu-
ality and licentiousness), not in quarreling and
jealousy. But clothe yourself with the Lord Jesus
Christ (the Messiah), and make no provision for
[indulging] the flesh [put a stop to thinking
about the evil cravings of your physical nature]
to [gratify its] desires (lusts).*

Romans 13:12-14

When I began to see a counselor five years into being a Christian, I was still a little amazed that I had even
considered it. I had been sure that God was all I needed to
get through whatever struggles I might have. I figured He
would show me what was wrong. But when I became
miserable enough, I went through with the first appoint-
ment and began a process that changed my life.

My first insight into the problem came with the

counselor's proclamation that I was in pretty bad shape. As an experienced counselor with a few personal trials that would stand your hair on end, she declared me severely depressed and one of the most emotionally abused people she'd ever known. With that diagnosis, she pointed out that the centerpiece of my problems was my rage and anger toward the agents of that abuse.

Some months into the process, she told me the really bad news: I was going to have to forgive all of those people. My first thought was, "No way!" It really made me angry. Why should *I* forgive *them*? The practical answer was pretty clear. It wasn't ruining their day that I hadn't forgiven them, but it was killing me. Still, I was definitely not in the recovery game to hand out forgiveness. Besides, I don't remember any of them saying they were sorry or asking for my forgiveness. And how would some of those people even ask for forgiveness when I would never see them again and couldn't find them if I wanted to?

Basically, I didn't want to do any work. I had signed up for counseling to be fixed. I wanted to be understood and given some kind of get-out-of-jail-free card for the misery in my heart. I didn't want to stop hating anyone or forgive people who didn't deserve to be forgiven. Couldn't my counselor just give me a pill? Couldn't I just learn some anger-management techniques and make all the bad feelings go away?

After all the whining came the Holy Spirit's conviction: The rage that festered within me was Satan's torment brought on by my unforgiveness. I had been carrying a lot of it, for a lot of people, for a lot of years. The result was that *I* had done all the suffering. I had developed all sorts of behaviors and pursued all sorts of unhealthy distractions that separated me from my anger. Habits like overeating, watching television, and engaging in other deadend pursuits were out of control. I had occasionally had short-term success in controlling those urges, but the need to medicate the tormenting anger always won. I would always gain the weight back or return to whatever I had done before to get relief. [1]

Every attempt I made to change my behavior required a great deal of self-control. Worse, whenever I stopped a medicating behavior, I experienced torment without relief. It was always hell. When dieting, for instance, my desire to overeat never abated as I tried to hang on through one more pound of weight loss.

I was powerless against my self-destructive behavior. Or was I? Hadn't I allowed Satan a foothold? Hadn't I invoked the promise of God to turn me over to the tormentor? Couldn't I end it all by choosing to forgive?

Looking back, it seems strange that I spent five years committed to Christian doctrine, which is based on forgiveness, but never confronted my own unforgiveness. I had read all of the right verses and thought I was practicing forgiveness in my life. I had heard from the pulpit that forgiveness was part of the walk of believers, but at no time did I consider that I had monumental layers of resentment and, in some cases, pure hatred lodged in my heart.

So when the conviction fell on me, I didn't respond with a glib, "Oops, my mistake, everybody is forgiven. Let's all be friends!" It took many months and many rounds of self-righteous anger before I was able to forgive. The anger had become part of my identity, having evolved from initial justified anger to self-righteousness, resentment and hatred. Now it was time to let that part of me die so I could receive the new heart Christ had promised. It was time to bring glory to God through the act of forgiveness and end Satan's constant presence or foothold in my life that was robbing me of joy.

I remember the moment as if it were yesterday. I was all alone. I spoke forgiveness and blessing to the central antagonists in my life. I did it for me. I did it to be free. I did it to honor God. They never knew and still don't. As much as I wanted to extract an apology from each of them, the act of forgiveness was about getting my own spiritual house in order. I had to do it to end my torment and reclaim the ability to resist Satan when he tempted me. Before, he had always won. Now I had a fighting chance.

Know that I didn't immediately feel much different after speaking those words into the air. I simply spoke the words and, in faith, committed to believe them and behave as if the forgiveness were real. Amazingly, it became real! That angry part of my life died off. About six months later, I noticed that I could feel love toward those who had been the objects of my past anger. I had become someone new, rewired inside with more peace and joy.

My unwanted behaviors, particularly when it came to overeating, became less of a struggle. Although at times, it was a "two steps forward and one step back" experience, my progress was positive. I ultimately found that I was sustaining a lower weight. That change was not because I had exerted more discipline than before; it was because I had less desire to overeat. I had more peace and less angst to medicate with food. This was one victory in many that would come, and I am sure many more victories will be mine as I continue to seek the transformation God has in store for me.

Getting One's Spiritual House in Order

My frustration and failure to manage my destructive behaviors were the direct result of not having my spiritual house in order. The graduates of the drug program suffered from the same affliction. They could not vanquish their addictions until they were willing to explore the places in their heart that caused them. Like me, they needed to get their spiritual houses in order and thereby regain the authority over their lives that Christ desires for us.

Simply put, getting our spiritual houses in order means living a life that does not conflict with God's laws. If we oppose those laws, we will be filled with the promised torment and reap consequences that negatively affect our lives. Our hearts will continue to drive unwanted behavior until we conform to His laws. The extent that our spiritual house is in order determines the extent to which we can resist sin. As Paul advised the Colossians (underlined emphasis is mine):

> *So kill (deaden, deprive of power) the evil desire lurking in your members [those animal impulses and all that is earthly in you that is employed in sin]: sexual vice, impurity, sensual appetites, unholy desires, and all greed and covetousness, for that is idolatry (the deifying of self and other created things instead of God). It is on account of these [very sins] that the [holy] anger of God is ever coming upon the sons of disobedience (those who are obstinately opposed to the divine will), Among whom you also once walked, <u>when you were living in and addicted</u> to [such practices]. But now put away and rid yourselves [completely] of all these things: anger, rage, bad feeling toward others, curses and slander, and foulmouthed abuse and shameful utterances from your lips! Do not lie to one another, for you have stripped off the old (unregenerate) self with its evil practices, And have clothed yourselves with the new [spiritual self], which is [ever in the process of being] renewed and remolded into [fuller and more perfect knowledge upon] knowledge after the image (the likeness) of Him Who created it.*
>
> Colossians 3:5-10

Changing Hearts

Some of the men urgently wanted to change their lives and take on their heart issues. For them, Beth and I, along with her dad, a program staff counselor, offered the men one-on-one ministry time to help them identify and restore their places of spiritual disorder. Each three- to four-hour ministry session began with the men telling their life stories so that we could identify the root causes that drove their addictions. Typically, all they knew was that something was amiss and that the standard program offerings were not going to be enough. They had all faithfully studied and prayed, but were still suffering from symptoms such as troubled sleep, lack of energy, reluctance to read the Bible or inability to understand it, strife in their relationships, lack of control over their anger, and much more. Nearly all shared the urge to drop out or to get high when they left the facility on a pass, knowing that they might face a random drug test when they returned. Some had gone so far in their premeditation as to have brainstormed ways to foil the drug test.

The ministry time was structured to:

❖ Identify the origin of their torment

❖ Repent of breaking God's law and then commit to conform to it

❖ Repent of taking their emotional pain to the world instead of to God

❖ Repent of using and idolizing drugs

❖ Convey forgiveness to the men as Christ's ministers

❖ Proclaim the truth of who they are in the eyes and heart of God and Christ

"Heartbreaking" is the only word to describe the abuse these men had suffered, usually beginning in childhood and often perpetrated by immediate family members. The abuse these men had received, combined with the abuse they had delivered, was the source of anger and deep shame that burned like coals heaped upon their hearts. When we heard their stories, it was easy for us to understand why they became substance abusers. Their illicit medications were tools of survival. The pain of their lives led to desperate acts. Little of what they had done was right or defensible, and their pain provided no consolation to the victims left in their path, yet their actions could at least be understood as those of people who relied on godless solutions and lies of the world. None of us would want to be tested as these men were tested, because we too might be driven to commit the same socially unacceptable or illegal acts if we believed our sanity or survival depended on it. [2]

Our ministry sessions began with emotionally exhausting stories of unthinkable inhumanity. But their tears were eventually dried by forgiveness, repentance and truth, as they gave glory to God and started the process of healing. We sometimes left those encounters drained of emotional energy, but always invigorated by the break-throughs and moved by love for the men and for God, who was orchestrating their victories.

Results of these sessions were often visible even before we finished our ministry time. As we worked through each issue, the guys' forgiveness and repentance would build up steam, causing them to transform outwardly to reflect what was going on inside. You could see the weight of their burdens begin to lift. Eyes would brighten, posture would become more erect, and smiles would break through. They had been loved by God's people. And they were seeing how they could escape a life in shambles by rebuilding their spiritual house.

In the days immediately following our sessions, nearly all the men reported manifestations of their improving spiritual house. As we worked with them to bring their hearts in line with God's law, their discomforts began to fade, making room for the transformation to begin. Their most troubling symptoms expressed before the one-on-one ministry time were either drastically improved or gone altogether.

One man reported he had not slept more than a few hours a night for 20 years and, as a result, suffered from anxiety and health problems. The morning after his time with us he slept in, missed breakfast, and had to be awakened for mid-morning class. His sleep was deep and restful for the first time in two decades, and he delighted in reporting over the next months that he now regularly "slept like a baby."

Another man had struggled with reading and understanding Scripture. His counselor would have him read a short passage and try to relate what it said immediately after reading it. He was totally unable to connect his thoughts or even repeat what he had just read. This was not true of other materials he read, only the Bible. It was more elusive than reading a foreign language, because no amount of study would allow him to comprehend or retain it. The day after our one-on-one time, he eagerly demonstrated to his counselor that he could now readily understand and retain the Word. When we would see him periodically in the following months, he would discuss his recent insights from Scripture and even quote passages relevant to our conversations.[3]

These men had advanced to a place where they were experiencing the presence of Satan less and feeling the presence of God more. Where they had once felt they had little hope for relief from their personal torment other than resorting to drugs, they now knew they had a fighting chance. Their hearts became more aligned with God's, and they were incredibly grateful for the time we spent with them.

The torment of what had been done to them and what they had done to others no longer drove them. That measure of freedom allowed the transformation process to *begin*. The transformation in their lives had begun, but they were not done. These men now had a chance to be transformed by the new ideas and practices of their Christian faith. Their minds and hearts were open to understanding God's wishes for their lives. Armed with God's truth and freed from a portion of their torment, they had the ability to make choices that would transform them into different people. They could now begin to live in alliance with their heart and not in conflict with it. They had become available for God, working through the Holy Spirit, to rewire them and eventually take away the previously irresistible temptation to use drugs.

Medical Causes of Addiction

Many people today subscribe to the concept that addicts have an addiction gene or a disease. This theory is appealing to addicts and enablers, because it blames bad behavior on physical causes, rather than personal choices. No one has to accept responsibility for addiction that's caused by a gene or disease. Plus, if there is a medical cause, then there is hope for a pill-like solution that doesn't require doing any heart-work to get free of the addiction. Competing theories suggest that no one knows whether addiction has a medical cause or not, but what I do know is the theory has provided an enabling crutch for many addicts, convincing them that their addictions are not their fault.

I remember grasping at a similar straw in my childhood. My parents wanted me to be a normal, slim, fit child. They understood the pain I felt as an obese child, who was often the target of "fat boy" abuse. When I was about eight years old, my physician father mentioned that a medical condition called overactive thyroid might be the source of the problem. I distinctly remember my reaction to that possibility: I became positively joyous. It was literally one of the happiest days of my childhood. Here was the end to all my shame of being fat. It wasn't my fault! All of the ridicule and inhumane hazing from my peers and others would stop. If my dad's hunch proved true, my shame would be eliminated!

Best of all, the remedy for an overactive thyroid was a pill! No more diets! No more being hounded by parents and others telling me not to eat so much. I soon would be able to eat as much as it seemed all of the other kids ate. To me, they all seemed to eat without bounds. They always had something in their mouths, yet they somehow maintained the body-type and the athleticism I wanted. So in one swift stroke of diagnosing a condition and fixing it with a pill, my life would be made right. I would pop a pill and be free of my shame and of the consequences of overeating forever!

Not so fast. The test results showed that I had an extraordinarily healthy thyroid.

You can see why disease and gene theories do not help addicts get free. All addicts would love for them to be true. I would have loved to discover that there is a fat gene. Others want proof there is a homosexual gene or a wife-beater gene or a pedophile gene or a compulsive shopping gene or a sports addiction gene. It would be great news in the battle against destructive behaviors that plague our society. The world would love it. No shame, no responsibility, and the hope for an instant medical cure.

The truth is that there *is* a "gene" for all of those behaviors. Call it a "flesh gene." And we all have it. It represents the latent potential for any sinful behavior that can be activated by our hearts. If our hearts are subjected to enough torment, bringing with it emotional pain, the flesh gene kicks in, activating sin to medicate the abuse. The sins we choose vary based on our training by others or our living environment. Of course, we can always choose God's answer for the torment.

An Addict's Story

I became acquainted with an addict who believed in the disease theory. It was evident from our conversation that the idea of addiction as a disease had allowed him to deal with his shame from being an alcoholic for most of his life. His addiction had harmed many people. Most disturbing were the family members who had become addicts and led very painful lives as a direct result of his addiction. He had also conned or stolen from family and friends to support his habit. All of this was made bearable for his conscience by believing that a disease was to blame for the behavior. He had never really owned the consequences of his actions because, under the disease theory, he was not responsible. Since he didn't take responsibility, he put forth no effort to address the cause of his addiction.

While he did become involved with AA and remained sober for over 20 years, he never advanced beyond sobriety. Certainly achieving sobriety was no small feat, but he was never free of the addiction and the need to go to AA meetings twice or even three times a week. He was never free of the desire to drink and never attained a quality of life beyond existing in a daily survival mode.

I came to know him in the final months of his life. One day, he told me his parents had gone to great lengths to communicate to him that his life was a mistake. They made it clear he would have been aborted had the procedure been available in the 1930s. They told him that his birth had cursed their lives. He had never forgiven them, but he believed he had dealt with his unforgiveness in a Christian way because he didn't think of them with anger or bitterness. In his parents' later years, he had even led the effort among his siblings to provide good care for his parents until their deaths.

One amazing night, as we were sitting in his den

talking about forgiveness, he decided to forgive his dad for nearly killing him at the age of five for spilling water at the dinner table. As punishment, his father had held his face in a bucket of water until his lungs screamed for air. It was a horrifying story, but just one of many terrible events in his life. We said a forgiveness prayer for his mom and dad. He asked God to forgive them for all of the abuse and to bless them wherever they were in death. He asked for God's mercy, not knowing how his prayer would fit into their passing and the mysterious mercies of God. In short, he put his spiritual house in order.

At that time, he had cancer but expected to live a little while longer. During these final months of his life, he drew closer and closer to God. He told me of Jesus coming into his bedroom and talking to him. He had dreams that revealed more places in his spiritual house he needed to get in order. One dream revealed to him that he needed to repent of a pornography idol. And there were many more dreams that ultimately brought him comfort as his death approached. When he prayed to God, their conversations were rich and full of life. His prayers were answered. Physical pain was removed upon his request of the Creator in the name of Jesus. He became a man transformed. He no longer rationalized his life by blaming an addiction gene or espousing an addiction disease theory. In the last months of his 68 years, he could finally claim to be free from addiction.

The hope of an addiction gene or disease did for him what the hope of a thyroid disorder did for me. It provided an easy way out, the hope of a quick, shame-free, no-accountability solution. It gave both of us something else to blame so we could avoid the work required to be free of our sin.

A Spiritual Perspective on Addiction

No group of people I have ever worked with has been more afflicted, more in bondage, or suffered more than the men in the program. As they walked off that stage on graduation day, those men were all saved, but they were not all healed, and they were not all delivered. The heart issues fueling the self-destructive behaviors that brought them to the drug program in the first place were still active. The heart will always succeed in revealing itself, in spite of whatever routine we wrap around it. An addicted heart will continue to drive addiction until it is transformed. The heart may change its drug of choice from alcohol to food or candy, TV or smoking, romance novels or pornography, sports or working, but it will not cease to desire medication.

We must get our spiritual house in order to allow the transformation in our hearts that will help us eliminate unwanted behaviors.

If you are like me, you came into Christianity with a commitment to give your life to Christ because He is the true Son of God, who was crucified and resurrected on the third day to break sin's death grip on our lives. We entered the relationship expecting the promises and power of God to manifest themselves in our lives. Yet, we brought a lot of manifested sin into this "marriage." Many of these sins were highly refined and had become part of our self-image and our identity. We did not realize that to experience the blessings God had for us, that person would have to go. We would have to plan a funeral for that old self to get the life we were really after.

The fundamental truth is that when our spiritual house is not in order, we are not really in control. So if we can't stop doing things like dipping tobacco, smoking, or controlling other obsessions, we need to look deeper into our hearts. If we can't demonstrate godly characteristics, like loving our neighbors or treating our families better without a great deal of effort, that is probably due to a conflict within our heart.

Scripture is clear that certain standards of behavior are expected of Christians. We are expected to demonstrate who we are in Christ and bring glory to God. It's self-evident that if Scripture tells us to take certain actions, then we have the ability to do so or to learn how to do so. As Paul told the Corinthians:

> *For no temptation (no trial regarded as enticing to sin), [no matter how it comes or where it leads] has overtaken you and laid hold on you that is not common to man [that is, no temptation or trial has come to you that is beyond human resistance and that is not adjusted and adapted and belonging to human experience, and such as man can bear]. But God is faithful [to His Word and to His compassionate nature], and He [can be trusted] not to let you be tempted and tried and assayed beyond your ability and strength of resistance and power to endure, but with the temptation He will [always] also provide the way out (the means of escape to a landing place), that you may be capable and strong and powerful to bear up under it patiently.*
>
> 1 Corinthians 10:13

If we are not able to control our actions and accomplish God's wishes, then we must remodel our spiritual house (heart) to resemble Christ's. Only when our foundation is aligned with God's Kingdom can we accomplish His will.

Dynamics of Self-Destructive Behavior Driven by Sin

We are the vessels in which the Holy Spirit dwells. When we disobey the laws of God, there are consequences.

When we obey, there are rewards. The emotional consequences of disobedience come in the form of intensely
negative feelings, or some kind of dis-ease. If these feelings
are bad enough, we will begin to find ways to escape our
dis-ease through some type of activity. Sometimes we will
become so dependent on that activity that we are unable to
control it, commonly progressing up the intensity scale if
the underlying torment is not dealt with. As the consequences of our medicating activities build up, we often
respond by increasing the activity or adopting other bad
habits.[4]

Stopping the behavior is a start, but dealing with the
torment that motivates it is the key to putting your spiritual
house in order.

Here are some things that indicate your house is out
of order:

❖ Unforgiveness

❖ Sexual immorality or perversion

❖ Drug usage

❖ Divorce

❖ Judging or condemning others

❖ Murder

❖ Any involvement with a false god or the occult

❖ Greed

❖ Gossip

❖ Gluttony

❖ Lying

❖ Stealing

What tempts us to let our house get out of order?
As I have observed through my own experience and work-

ing with others, there are two levels of temptation.

1. Temptation driven by the sin nature
2. Temptation driven by torment

Consider the flesh temptation that is common to man. There are many behaviors we are warned against as being impure or ungodly. If we choose to give in to those sins, there will be consequences, not the least of which is that it serves Satan's purposes and grieves the Holy Spirit living within you. The results will at least be guilt, shame, and a sense that you have distanced yourself from God. If a sin becomes habitual, worse consequences are likely to follow. The results of things like gluttony, sexual perversion, lying, and stealing are obvious.

All sin has two levels of consequence: spiritual and physical. On a spiritual level, sin negatively affects your relationship with God, Jesus and the Holy Spirit. It also brings glory to Satan and advances his kingdom.

On a physical level, sin is followed by feelings of shame, physiological repercussions, or legal consequences. For instance, gluttony can lead to obesity and related health problems. Sex outside of marriage can bring on health problems, stir up emotional turmoil, and negatively affect intimacy in marriage. Stealing, sometimes driven by covetousness, could get you jail time. Lying about it could get you more.

Some Christians say, "Why worry about sin? Isn't that why Jesus died on the cross?" Yes, He did, but that was to free us from an eternity of hell and give us access to His Kingdom *right now*. In return, we are to refrain from sinning to honor Him and His sacrifice. To do otherwise is to mock His act of love and create for ourselves a version of hell on earth. Remember that God loves us perfectly and desires that we be full of the light and the joy of His Son. He knows the high price we pay for sinning. He has warned us about the "wages of sin" just as any loving father would warn a child he dearly loves. [5]

As James spells out in his letter:

> *But every person is tempted when he is drawn away, enticed and baited by his own evil desire (lust, passions). Then the evil desire, when it has conceived, gives birth to sin, and sin, when it is fully matured, brings forth death.*
>
> James 1:14 -15

Other than the temptation common to all, the second type of temptation is driven by intense heartfelt discomfort that is tormenting. Refusing to forgive is one of the most common sources of torment. In these situations, bitterness, anger, and overall emotional angst will just not go away. At this point, the Lord's promise to turn us over to the tormentor has occurred. Unforgiveness is an affront to the redemptive act of Christ. It opposes everything God has called us to be. So I can see why He wants us to be very uncomfortable when this happens.

When we are faced with the need to forgive, we can go one of two ways. We can refuse to forgive, which intensifies sinful temptations as we seek to escape our heart's angst. Or we can put our spiritual house back in order and end the torment by forgiving. As I have witnessed in myself and others, the decision to medicate the pain can lead us to become dependent on sinful behavior to cool the torment, even to the point that we choose friends, neighborhoods, jobs and activities that support the behavior.

A Life Change is Required

To be free of an unwanted behavior, we not only have to put our spiritual house in order, but we must change our lives so that the unwanted behavior is starved off. We must reduce the pull of the behavior to the point that it can be resisted. Because the life patterns we develop around a sin support the sin and will continue to do so even after the torment has been removed, we must be willing to give up our old life in order to be totally free. To eliminate influences that perpetuate unwanted behaviors, you need to soberly examine the following aspects of your life:

❖ Where you live

❖ Your friends

❖ Other sins that support the out-of-control behavior

❖ Books you read

❖ Songs you listen to

❖ Your job

❖ Movies you see

❖ TV shows you watch

❖ Your romantic relationships

❖ Your route home

❖ Any aspect of your life

This is just a sample. The point is that we must be willing to give up everything that supports our sin. In our ministry, we once had a situation where someone had remained drug free until he returned home and sat in a certain chair where he used to get high. He couldn't resist the strong connection between the place and the behavior.

To support the person I was trying to be, here are some of the decisions I made:

- ❖ Watched only G- or PG-rated movies
- ❖ Read no more books that were so intense that they removed me from my reality
- ❖ Quit listening, singing, or playing in my head any music other than praise music
- ❖ Moved to a different state when getting married
- ❖ Discontinued relationships that did not support my new life
- ❖ Avoided job opportunities that would require regular contact with co-workers or customers who might drag me back into my old habits.
- ❖ Quit watching TV for awhile, later added science and history channels, plus the news

A Hard Message to Those Who are Uncommitted

The reaction I got from the men in the program when I made such suggestions was shock and protest. It was clear they were not going to make the life changes required to support the temporary sobriety they had achieved at the program. Think about this for a minute. Even though some of these guys hadn't been sober for years they would not consider altering their life enough to stay that way.

The Proof that Sobriety Does Not Equal Transformation

For the men in the recovery program, there was nothing there that supported their old selves or their old habits. Many reported that they had no temptation to use while in residence. The obvious correlation between the program lifestyle and their sobriety did not convince them that they needed to make radical life changes to stay sober. Most men went back to their old lives and were reunited with their old addictions.

That is compelling evidence of two things. First, our lives, down to the details of our routine, support our behavior. The old life must become transformed into a new life that will support the new behavior. Second, anyone who is unwilling to change his life to be free of addiction desires a quick fix and will fail. Most of the men were there to be fixed and then return to their old life hoping that it would work this time.

Transformation Applies to More than Addiction

As a reminder, this book is not about addiction. It is just that ministry to the addicted was the context in which I had the discernment about God's call for transformation. God's call is for *all* of us to be transformed from what we are, into what He wants us to be. By getting your house in order, spiritually and physically, you can accomplish that change.

If there is anything you do not like about yourself, you can overcome it by responding to His call. Anything. Because when you respond to the call, you are on a path to becoming more like Jesus. The more you are like Jesus, the more you will love the Father, and the more you will sense and understand His love for you. And you will love His law like Jesus does. In that process, the root of any unwanted behavior or condition that resides in your heart will be addressed.

Take the First Step

Whether you are tormented by the shame and self-condemnation brought on by all sin or you are under torment from invoking specific consequences, consider taking the first step toward getting your spiritual house in order. If you are like most of us, you are probably suffering from some degree of unforgiveness toward someone. Let me encourage you to go before the Lord in prayer and ask Him to show you who you need to forgive. It could be someone that abused you or the last person that cut you off in traffic. It is not required that the person ever knows that they have been forgiven. It is an issue of the heart, and it is *your* heart. Speak forgiveness to that person in prayer and pray specific blessings for them in Jesus' name. This is all about using the reconciling power of Jesus to free you from a dark place of bitterness and unforgiveness. It is exactly what Jesus did for you!

Supporting Scripture References:

1. "...not in fleshly wisdom but by the grace of God (the unmerited favor and merciful kindness by which God, exerting His holy influence upon souls, turns them to Christ, and keeps, strengthens, and increases them in Christian virtues)."   2 Corinthians 1:12

2. "Confess to one another therefore your faults (your slips, your false steps, your offenses, your sins) and pray [also] for one another, that you may be healed and restored [to a spiritual tone of mind and heart]. The earnest (heartfelt, continued) prayer of a righteous man makes tremendous power available [dynamic in its working]."   James 5:16

3. "So get rid of all uncleanness and the rampant outgrowth of wickedness, and in a humble (gentle, modest) spirit receive and welcome the Word which implanted and rooted [in your hearts] contains the power to save your souls."
                                        James 1:21

4. "Do you not discern and understand that you [the whole church at Corinth] are God's temple (His sanctuary), and that God's Spirit has His permanent dwelling in you [to be at home in you, collectively as a church and also individually]?"   1 Corinthians 3:16

5. "What shall we say [to all this]? Are we to remain in sin in order that God's grace (favor and mercy) may multiply and overflow? Certainly not! How can we who died to sin live in it any longer? Are you ignorant of the fact that all of us who have been baptized into Christ Jesus were baptized into His death?"   Romans 6:1-3

Chapter Eight

The Truth About Lies

And you will know the Truth, and the Truth will set you free.

John 8:32

"**Stupid**, ugly, unlovable and worthless best describe what I believed to be true about myself as an eight-year-old." This opening line from the first chapter exposes the lies that not only shaped my childhood, but affected a lot of my adult life. Living a life without God cut me off from the truth that would have opposed the lies lodged in my heart. Who I believed myself to be powerfully and negatively impacted the quality of my existence.

I didn't know until God began to transform me that pursuing His Truth would change my self-image on a heart level. Nor did I realize it would be necessary to conform to His Laws *and* replace the lies I believed about myself with His truth to eliminate the torment that motivated my temptation to medicate. In fact, both are required for transformation.

Just as we have done in our personal transformations, Beth and I have helped many other people confess and repent of the sin that brought them a negative consequence and confront the lies that caused them grief. For instance, in our ministry we commonly encounter people whose fathers never said "I love you." Often they resent their fathers for this and believe lies about themselves because of it. "Unlovable," "unworthy of love," or "too bad to be loved" are the kinds of messages they have internalized. Angry and hurt, their wounded hearts have influenced them to make damaging life choices.

To heal the heartache that comes from believing they are not lovable, people must work through a three-step process. First they must do the work of forgiveness. Second, they must reject the lies they've come to believe. Third, they must substitute God's Truth for the lies that have been fed to them. The truth is that all followers of Christ are chosen and loved by God perfectly. Period.

Father of Lies

The things we believe about ourselves directly affect the course and quality of our lives. A reality full of lies promotes Satan's agenda. He wants you to live a life of hell on earth fueled by as many lies as he can get you to accept. **Every** lie you encounter is from Satan and advances his purposes. Jesus clearly identified this connection when He spoke to the religious rulers:

> *He (Satan) was a murderer from the beginning and does not stand in the truth, because there is no truth in him. When he speaks a falsehood, he speaks what is natural to him, for he is a liar [himself] and the father of lies and of all that is false.*

> John 8:44

That doesn't leave much room for interpretation. We can also be assured that if a lie has taken up residence in our hearts, it will be the source of emotional distress, because it is something Satan would like us to believe about our life. That's why, in the transformation process, we must not only confront our heart-level opposition to God's laws, we must free our hearts of lies. When we extract a lie from our hearts and replace it with the Truth, we can reap God's blessing. And God has a powerful Truth to oppose every lie we may believe about ourselves. As pointed out by John in his gospel, God has not and will not ever utter a lie.

> *Whoever receives His testimony has set his seal of approval to this: God is true. [That man has definitely certified, acknowledged, declared once and for all, and is himself assured that it is divine truth that God cannot lie].*
>
> John 3:33

Lies Curse

What if someone who's important to you says that you are a loser and that nothing is going to go right for you, starting now? Let's say that you have always looked up to this person and have often asked for his advice. Chances are that you will either completely or partially accept what he has said as true. We certainly had guys in rehab who had been told by people important in their lives that they were never going to have victory over their addiction. Lies like those become self-fulfilling prophecies of doom, producing the same result as a curse.

Believing false labels or false predictions of failure also can be a curse. The position of Alcoholic Anonymous (AA), for example, is that there is no cure for alcoholism. If you are an alcoholic in AA and believe that, you have just signed on for a life of unrelenting temptation to drink self-destructively. Jesus did not come back to set the captives free of every type of bondage except alcoholism. If an alcoholic believes he is a "drunk," he will make decisions that support that lie and may give up trying to get truly free. If someone believes that he is unlovable, he will interpret his world accordingly and make choices that fit the label.

Lies also tend to perpetuate "curses" by resisting the evidence of opposing truth. I knew a man who believed he was unlovable. That false label made him feel isolated and lonely. That message was ingrained in him as a result of the cruelty he experienced during his early years. As a Christian adult, he had sleepless nights that degenerated into tears of rejection and desperate pleas to the darkness for someone to love him. It was heartbreaking, especially to his wife of several years, who would roll over and reassure him that she loved him and remind him that his life included meaningful friendships and a fulfilling job where he was respected and valued. But it made no difference. In times of quiet when there were no distractions, the lies successfully challenged the truth and kept him in a state of intermittent misery. He eventually overcame his misery, first by forgiving the people responsible for the lie and then by rejecting the lie itself. Now, by believing the truth that God loves him unconditionally, he is able to accept the love of others on a deep heart level.

Living the truth

Living with new truth may sound easy enough, but it requires discipline to dispel old lies. Familiar belief systems affect our responses to life events, and take time and effort to break. When we live with a lie for a long time, it becomes like a well developed muscle that has the strength to affect you emotionally. When exposed by the Truth we need to allow lies to atrophy while we learn to trust the Truth.

Suppose you go to the doctor for back pain and find out your problem is caused by the way you lift heavy objects. The doctor refers you to a physical therapist who helps you to build the right muscles for lifting and to retrain your body not to use the over-developed muscle that causes back pain when you lift. Despite knowing the truth about how to lift pain free, you will fight to overcome your lifelong conditioning to use the wrong muscle. Also, the new muscle will not lift as much until it has had a chance to develop. So you will have to resist the temptation to use the wrong muscle, even when it is expedient.

The point is that living a new life under new truth will take some getting used to. You can expect old lies to tempt you to return to familiar beliefs and habits. This is once again Satan's scheme to lure you into believing lies, knowing that you are more easily tricked with lies you have believed before. In his letter to the Ephesian church, Paul calls for a life of spiritual maturity based on truth that honors Christ.

Rather, let our lives lovingly express truth [in all things, speaking truly, dealing truly, living truly]. Enfolded in love, let us grow up in every way and in all things into Him Who is the Head, [even] Christ (the Messiah, the Anointed One)
Ephesians 4:15

The Sources of Lies

So where do the lies come from? Practically everywhere. They can come from outside sources or from within ourselves. While all lies originate with Satan, they reach us through many channels. Let's look at four main sources of lies.

1. Shared lies

Shared lies occur when someone you come in contact with shares a false reality, either by example or by expressing an opinion on some aspect of life. Whenever we come in contact with others, the potential exists for us to be exposed to the lies they live under. If we accept their way of life or their perspective, we risk adopting their lies, too. In the drug program, we often witnessed men being influenced by expressed beliefs or examples set by the other men. The false realities ranged from believing superstitions on how to beat the random drug test to claiming to know someone else's motives, which would require mind reading. Unfortunately, we are all just as likely as those men to accept the things our peers practice or preach if they seem plausible or serve our needs.

2. Authority lies

Authority figures may also share false beliefs or opinions that could have a life-changing impact on us. We often allow influential people to speak authoritatively into our lives because of their position or knowledge. People such as coaches, teachers, bosses, or government officials are a few of those who have authority because of position. Doctors, pastors and counselors have subject-matter authority, and we seek them out for help. When we respect someone's authority, it tends to make our hearts more open to accepting what they say as true and possibly believing lies.

Family members have the ability to speak into our lives in an even more powerful way. Parents top the list of influencers because of their family authority. Fathers, with their responsibility and accountability to Jesus for the spiritual health of the family, have significant influence on the reality of everyone in the family. The words fathers speak over their children have the power to impact the course of their lives. From our ministry experience, Beth and I have discovered that, while mother's words carry significant weight, it is the things that fathers say or fail to say to their children that seem to have the greatest impact on their beliefs about themselves. Many of the men we

ministered to in the drug program were living under negative messages from their fathers that had clearly influenced
the outcome of their lives. Being told they were worthless,
lazy, a failure, or stupid was very common.

When fathers are not available for their children,
emotionally or physically, the children may grow up inter-
nalizing painful messages like:

 ❖ I don't love you.

 ❖ You are unlovable.

 ❖ You are not important to me.

 ❖ You are unimportant.

Now the fathers of these men were probably just reflecting
the messages they grew up under, but that circumstance
does not reduce any of the emotional pain suffered by their
own children.

When a father makes a negative pronouncement
about his child in the presence of others, the impact is
greater and more hurtful to the child. During the writing of
this chapter, I witnessed an example of this while standing
in the check-out line of a department store. The man in
front of me fielded a request from his middle-school-aged
son, which was delivered loudly across 30 feet or so of
checkout counters.

"Dad, can we get this?" the boy asked, holding up a
mesh bag full of practice golf balls.

"No," replied the father. "You lost all the ones you
had, and I am not buying any more."

The boy lifted the bag a little higher and beseech-
ingly delivered his most compelling response to overcome
the objection: "Dad, I promise to be careful to not lose
these if we get them."

By now, about 25 people were fully engaged in this
very public "fathering moment," which ended when the

father responded, "Well, you are a habitual liar and can't tell the truth, so put 'em back!"

Imagine the boy's shame and heartache at being publicly labeled a habitual liar by one of the most influential and authoritative people in his life. Unless the father later asked the boy's forgiveness and proclaimed the truth, his son will one day have to work through forgiving his dad, rejecting the lie, and substituting the truth. If the boy were only to forgive his dad, he would still suffer under the label of "liar."

3. Cultural lies

Our culture disseminates propaganda that flies in the face of God's message about who we are, how we got here, and how we should act. The range of lies runs from "sex outside of marriage is enlightened thinking" to "your value as a person is based on how you look or how much money you have." Just being alive exposes us to constant messages that oppose God's truth. Cultural influences are powerful and insidious and should be presumed guilty of lying unless proven innocent. Enough said.

4. Self inflicted lies

Most people probably don't know that they are living under self-inflicted lies. These lies are things that we come to believe by misinterpreting the meaning of an experience. We reach conclusions and make assumptions all the time as we go about the business of living. We really could not function if we did not make some assumptions, which may unavoidably lead to false conclusions. Life forces us to guess about a lot of things, especially when it comes to understanding the motivation and meaning of what others have done.

As humans, we have the self-destructive tendency to believe things about ourselves that aren't true, such as believing that if our parents don't say they love us, they don't. Or believing that if someone is not as talkative as usual, he or she is angry with us. Or believing that there's something wrong with us when we don't get a job offer after an interview. Or believing that our teacher doesn't like us because we failed a test.

Making wrong assumptions usually leads to accepting false conclusions about ourselves as truth. And it is more likely to happen if we already believe one or more lies. Every lie sets us up to believe more lies. In the case of the student who thinks the teacher doesn't like her personally because of her failed test, the student may have reached that conclusion because she already believed that adults don't like her. Whenever there is a gross overreaction to what should be a fairly benign incident it is a sign to start looking for a heartfelt lie that's causing that person to misinterpret his or her world.

The presence of a lie in our hearts will not only oppose the truth, it may also affirm what is false. The coach I mentioned in the first chapter who announced in class practically every day that my only value was to melt and reduce the price of lard is a good example. Because I had already allowed messages into my heart that supported his proclamation, his opinion reinforced my feelings of worthlessness. I can't remember for sure, but I don't think I ever told my parents about the verbal abuse, or even considered doing so, although it continued for months. I didn't even offer to tell them about the beating the coach gave me. It only came out at dinner that night when I was asked why sitting down caused such obvious pain. What the coach said and did were just different expressions of familiar treatment. As such, this episode just wasn't particularly remarkable to me. His lies fit into my reality, and I had no guard against it.

The Lie within the Offense

Lies usually don't become a part of our self-perception without the help of someone we probably need to forgive. A lie that affects us this way starts as a message we receive, either from a specific statement or from how we are treated. If we choose to believe the stated or implied message, it becomes a part of our self-image and will impair our quality of life until it is removed. As discussed earlier, to end our emotional torment we must forgive the offenders in our lives, because God's law requires it. Then we must identify and reject the lies that have lodged in our heart, because they are from Satan and will cause suffering. A lie is a dark gift that keeps on giving. Forgiving alone will not remove the torment of a lie if we continue to believe it.

Lies and Offenses Work Together

Let's use a common driving situation to illustrate how lies are built into offenses. Someone cuts in front of you to make a turn instead of first slowing down to let you pass. You are angry about the driver's rudeness. But what is it about the situation that creates an offense that angers you? Was the other driver acting out of concern for you? No. In fact, you were put at risk for his convenience. Thus, the driver communicated that his need for convenience is more important than your need for safety. Your choice is either to accept that message as true or, hopefully, with your healthy self-esteem, to reject it as a lie and go on with your life unaffected. If you do not guard your heart in such situations, you could receive and accept as part of your self-image that you are not important or that you have less value than others. You know to forgive the driver, but if you have accepted the driver's message as true, you have accepted a lie into your heart.

Here is a situation based on a real event. A 10-year-old victim is kidnapped. She is tied up, blindfolded, tossed into the trunk of a car, and driven to a distant location where she is sexually abused by her female captor. This event sparked a life-long tail spin into drug usage, which leads one to wonder what lies were tormenting her. What did she come to believe as true about herself as a result of the incident? Here are some possibilities:

- ❖ I am a homosexual.
- ❖ It will happen again.
- ❖ I will always be a victim.
- ❖ I am powerless.
- ❖ There is something wrong with me.
- ❖ I deserved it for my sins.
- ❖ God hates me.
- ❖ I will not be able to marry and have a normal family.
- ❖ I am damaged goods.
- ❖ The shame of what happened will never go away.

All of these lies and more haunted the victim and were medicated with drugs.

How to Combat Lies

1. Know the Truth

The best way to identify lies is to know the truth. That's accomplished by continually reinforcing the truth, so that any lie presents a stark contrast. I have heard that the most effective way to train currency inspectors to detect counterfeit tender is to constantly expose them to genuine money. It has been discovered that when inspectors study counterfeit money, they are actually less likely to identify bogus currency.

It is the same with the Truth of God. *The more we know His Truth, the more likely we are to discern a lie from Satan.* It does require an investment in time, but knowing what God thinks is the standard we must use to create the life we want. The more that we dig into Scripture and allow God to inform us of His character, the easier it is to identify the lies we live with.

Paul declares the value of knowing God to the Philippians when he said:

> . . . *I count everything as loss compared to the possession of the priceless privilege (the overwhelming preciousness, the surpassing worth, and supreme advantage) of knowing Christ Jesus my Lord and of progressively becoming more deeply and intimately acquainted with Him [of perceiving and recognizing and understanding Him more fully and clearly]. For His sake I have lost everything and consider it all to be mere rubbish (refuse, dregs), in order that I may win (gain) Christ (the Anointed One),*
>
> Philippians 3:8

As an example, consider someone whose ambition is to become an expert on George Washington. From studying his writing and actions, she learns where he stood on the issues of his time. Eventually, she feels as if she understands how Washington thought, as if she "knows" him. Historians are commonly asked what an historical figure might do about a current problem, such as "What would Washington do about global warming?" The answer is inferred from "knowing" Washington. In the same way, it dawned on me soon after becoming a Christian to test the rightness of ideas and actions against the personality of

God. If something did not fit with who I believed God, Jesus and the Holy Spirit to be, then I rejected it. I didn't spend time studying Satan's ways so I could identify lies.

Scripture not only tells us a lot about how we are regarded by God, it also provides an understanding of His personality and character. When there is not a specific scripture passage that provides the answer we need, we can get a pretty good idea of God's answer if we "know" Him. As we seek to know the God of the universe through His Word, we will clearly perceive the lies with which Satan assaults us.

2. Guard Your Heart

We can always rely on the infallible Heavenly Father to speak the truth. With everyone else we need to guard our heart. Paul cautions the early church to test even prophetic words and inspired teaching, and to guard our hearts in these letters to the New Testament church.

Do not spurn the gifts and utterances of the prophets [do not depreciate prophetic revelations nor despise inspired instruction or exhortation or warning]. But test and prove all things [until you can recognize] what is good; [to that] hold fast.

Thessalonians 5:20-21

Be alert and on your guard; stand firm in your faith (your conviction respecting man's relationship to God and divine things, keeping the trust and holy fervor born of faith and a part of it).

1 Corinthians 16:13

Just knowing the truth is not enough. We need to guard our hearts. That means we must always test what we hear from others and from ourselves against God's truth. When it comes to what people say about us or what we believe about ourselves, just ask yourself if it could have come from the heart of Jesus, someone who loves you so much that He died for you. He chose to sacrifice Himself rather than be separated from you for eternity. Take a moment to let that sink into your heart.

3. Reject Lies and Proclaim the Truth

Dispatching a lie and substituting the truth is not difficult. All you have to do is reject the lie and proclaim the truth in the name of Jesus. Here is an example for someone who believes they are unlovable:

> Heavenly Father, I reject the lie that I am unlovable and I proclaim the truth that You love me perfectly; that You have known me since the beginning of time and chose me to be with You for eternity. I proclaim this in the name of Jesus. Amen.

More Truth Equals More Transformation

When Jesus was tested by Satan, it is written that Satan found nothing of himself in Jesus. More specifically, nothing that resembles Satan exists in the heart of Jesus. Our objective is to increasingly have a heart like the heart of Christ. Lies are from Satan, so as we remove them, our hearts begin to look more like the heart of Jesus and become less familiar to Satan. The more our hearts are transformed to resemble the heart of Christ, the more we will share in His divine nature and power. Paul put it this way to the church in Ephesus:

> *And put on the new nature (the regenerate self) created in God's image, [Godlike] in true righteousness and holiness.*

Therefore, rejecting all falsity and being done now with it, let everyone express the truth with his neighbor, for we are all parts of one body and members one of another.

Ephesians 4:24-25

Chapter Nine

"Love Me More"

Therefore, my dearly beloved, shun (keep clear away from, avoid by flight if need be) any sort of idolatry (of loving or venerating anything more than God)
1 Corinthians 10:14

Several years ago I stood in front of the mirror checking out my stubborn, bulging middle feeling frustrated by the excess weight I still carried. I had been a Christian for 15 years and had been through several rounds of trying to drop those last 15 to 20 pounds, but never could for very long. While easily maintaining a weight 60 pounds less than my high, I was still in the familiar cycle of weight loss and weight gain, just on a smaller "scale." Not only was I tired of always worrying with this problem, I had always felt like it revealed a weakness in my faith. It seemed like an outward demonstration that I was not managing my temptations well, that something was amiss spiritually. My concern was that if others perceived my inability to stay slim as a flaw, they would be less likely to ask about my faith.

I just stood there poking, squeezing and rotating the evidence of my weakness. In a moment of pure candor, I did something unusual, speaking aloud this heartfelt petition: "Lord, why is it that after 15 plus years of being a Christian, and all you have done to give me a life worth living, why am I still struggling with my weight?"

I will never forget the response. I received an answer in the form of an impression so strong, it almost seemed as if someone was in the room. I even looked around, half expecting to see someone standing there. The simple answer was, "*Love me more.*"

My heart leapt at the truth, and it felt like I had an answer. It was a very stirring moment, as the strength of the revelation was powerful. Not totally sure what it meant, I resolved to understand and implement the response to my question.

However, as I processed the answer over the next week, I concluded that I had nothing. I simply didn't know *how* to love Him more. I already gave Him credit for all of the good things that had ever happened to me. When taking communion, worshiping, or praying, my heartfelt love for God always came through. I just really loved God, and didn't know how to love Him any more than I did. I began to think it was really just a works message – work harder, do more, pray more, read more, give more. Finally this "truth" was thrown into the "more bucket" with all the other lies about righteousness earned through works. I became uncertain this answer had come from God after all, and for a time I ignored it.

Two years later, while working with the men in drug rehab, a new interpretation of the message came to me. It was during the first days of trying to figure out why so many of them were failing that I realized their failures had a great deal to do with what they loved and why they loved it.

The Things We Love

How often have we all said and heard others say how much we love something like chocolate or fishing or shopping or watching sports? Our culture carelessly throws around the "love" word to make a point, or as a playful, engaging way to state a preference for something. In contrast, when someone in the rehab program tells you they love to get high, it's an ominous statement of fact. It's really hard to hear an addict say that repeatedly, especially when you realize it's not an exaggeration. Most of these guys really did love to get high. Despite all that they had suffered under the grip of their addiction and their sincere desire to quit, they commonly expressed a sincere love of getting high. What they hated and wanted to stop were the repercussions of their habit, not the sensation. Addicts don't go into treatment because they no longer like to get high. They go because of the destruction their addiction has caused. If there were a version of cocaine that did not destroy lives, a lot more people would be addicted.

God's Call to Love Him

During one of those many afternoons when I was meditating on what to say to the guys at Tuesday night chapel, I realized the message I had received that day in front of the mirror was absolutely right. But my interpretation had been absolutely wrong.

God was not calling me to love Him more than I already did, although I am sure that is also His desire. In answer to the question specifically regarding my weight, He was saying, "Love me more than you love food." Now that made sense! Although I had done a lot to get my spiritual house in order, this new understanding revealed another one of God's laws that I needed to address. His Scriptures are very clear on this: He wants us to love him more than anything else, period. [1]

Loving Anything More Than God

But why was my weight still a nagging problem, since there didn't seem to be anything driving me to overeat? I just did. And I did it frequently enough to sustain more weight than I wanted. The truth was that I really did behave toward food as if I loved it. When I considered how often food was on my mind relative to how much I thought about God, I could really see how out of balance my heart was.

That night at dinner with the family, as I blessed the meal, I repented of loving food more than God and asked for forgiveness. That was a tough thing to do. (More on humility later.) However, I knew that when God is honored and obeyed, there is victory.

I thought it important to do it at the dinner table, because I wanted my wife and two sons to witness the act of repentance by the one responsible to Christ for the spiritual health of the family. I believe as fathers and husbands we must be transparent about our struggle with sin and model repentance when appropriate. I believe that exposing our struggles and victories provides an empowering model for our family members' transformation journeys.

That night our dinner conversation was about how we allow things to become more important to us than our love for God. If we love anything of this world more than we love God, it hinders our Christian walk and influences our behavior in ways that prevent us from being Christ-like. Loving God more than anything else brings Him His deserved glory and bestows a blessing on us.

Immediately after that evening's meal, food had less of a hold on me, and I began to live out the intention of my repentance. Within a few months, I had dropped a couple of inches from my waistline. While the improvement was great, the more important result was that it helped me understand the sin of loving something more than loving God.

This experience also revealed that the guys in rehab and I shared yet another common condition of man. Many of those who had failed after graduation still loved to get high. They didn't love the addiction or the consequences, but they did love the part about being high. In their conversations about it, they sounded almost like love-struck teenagers who talk about the things they want to do and places they want to go with their new love interest. And just like teenagers, some would visibly perk up during these discussions. In the middle of their recovery, getting high still had a grip on their hearts.

We even witnessed some who grieved for their lost drug habit in the same way they might have grieved over the death of a loved one. After completing one-on-one ministry sessions with us, in which they repented of drug use, a few reported that they initially felt great about the time we spent together, but later they felt curiously sad, even tearing up spontaneously. This odd reaction sometimes went on for days. It was grief for the loss of something they had loved.

Delighting in God

God knows that we are led by our love, and He wants us to be drawn into relationship with Him. We are created to delight in Him, to be excited to know Him, and to be lifted up by His character and power and heart and all the things that make up His nature. Imagine someone's delighted excitement in purchasing a new car. You can just see the proud owner pointing out all of the great things about the engine, the color, the styling, the power, and the sound system. As they go through the list, they are ani-

mated, smiling, and sometimes giddy about their new car.
They are truly delighted by it. That is the way God wants us
to feel about and talk about Him. He would like for us to
be eager to show Him off, to demonstrate openly and
lovingly how much He delights us. And He wants us to
make time to be with Him. [2, 3]

The point is that even after we have gotten our
spiritual house in order and eliminated the tormenting
source of unwanted behavior, we still have to neutralize the
love we had for that behavior. Our sinful nature, when
combined with our love for the behavior, can still under-
mine our intentions to be free.

For example, the love of smoking can tempt a
former smoker to light up even though he really wants to
stay away from smoking for good. A reformed smoker once
told me that he loved practically everything about the
process of smoking. He loved the way the cigarette looked
in his hand, how cool he thought smoking made him
appear, blowing out the smoke, even the process of taking
out the cigarette and lighting up. This person just loved it
all. Fortunately his habit had not gone on long enough for
him to become chemically addicted, so when he decided
that the negatives of smoking were too great, he didn't love
it anymore and quit. In this situation, there was no physiological dependency to overcome; only the heart was hooked
to the behavior. It was purely driven by the love of the
experience.

Idols of the World

There is no blessing in loving worldly things. As Jesus told the Pharisees, "You shall love the Lord your God
with all your heart, and with all your soul, and with all your
mind. This is the greatest and first commandment." (Matthew 22:37-38) Loving anything more than God is idolatry,
and it violates His spiritual law. Just as loving God is a

blessing, loving things of the world is a curse.

Look at how hard it is to stop a self-destructive behavior that has hooked your heart. And while loving the world too much may not invite the same torment as unforgiveness, it has definite spiritual consequences, the least of which is being controlled by the object of our love. Are we better off pursuing a love relationship with the perfect Creator or inviting the world to put a ring in our nose and lead us around like a cow?

Loving God Guides a Blessed Life

At those moments of truth when we struggle with a decision that will either glorify the Lord or glorify the things of this world, love for the Lord helps us make the right choice. In my first years of Christianity, I was continually confronted with that type of decision. While I wanted to hold true to my new convictions, the pull of the old ways was still present and strong. There were times when I felt I could not make the right decision for myself, my wife, or my children, but I could often muster up the determination for God's sake.

I am grateful to God, and I love Him in a real way that is not easy for all to appreciate. I think the fact that I did not grow up in the church has been an advantage, because when I found God, I didn't see him through the prism of Sunday school teachings or church doctrine. For me, hearing the Word for the first time was like shock treatment, causing a radical conversion that led me to reject my old, godless life. I had lived a life that disregarded spiritual matters, and I had pursued the things of the world with a vengeance. I had a lot of feelings to medicate and passed up few opportunities to do so. When I came to the Lord, I was like a drowning man reaching for a life raft. My life had been miserable. I had tried everything I thought would finally bring me peace and joy, arriving at that point in life more than just empty handed. I was bankrupt. When I was able to hear the Word of God through the smoldering despair of my existence, the Truth truly set me free. God offered me a life worth living, and I love Him for it.

Through my imperfect and inconsistent pursuit of Him and His truth, I have achieved a quality of life far greater than mere survival. My life is increasingly full of joy and peace, and I give God all the credit. By my strength alone, it wasn't attainable. For this and other victories, I can declare to you here that I love God.

Loving God Will Bring a Transformed Heart and Life

If you are struggling to be free of self-destructive behavior or if you are sitting through church every Sunday, chained to a blasé lifeless faith, launch your emancipation by loving God and seeking out His truth in your life. Set your mind to putting your spiritual house in order and to loving nothing greater than you love God.

He Does the Transforming If We Conform to His Laws

To reach this new place in your life, combine the Bible reading and prayer that you are encouraged to do from the pulpit, with a commitment to become a new being in Christ. Remember, you have to own your transformation. There is nothing the pastor can do or say that will eliminate your responsibility to become transformed. Nor can he reduce the effort it will take you to get there.

Keep in mind that while we do have responsibility for our transformation, God will do the actual work of changing your heart. Our call is to love Him and live in accordance with His laws. As we do, He will do the heart-work that advances us down the road of transformation. And that road leads to a life free from worldly bondage to a place where we can cash in on the abundant life promised by God. [4, 5, 6]

Over the years, I've heard many people complain that the church doesn't feed them spiritually. While that may be true for them and for you, it is also true that we are responsible for feeding ourselves, for doing the work God has called us to do. No one can do it for us, and we cannot expect to live a powerful Christian life just because we are promised one as Christians. We have to pursue the changed heart of a new being to turn God's promises into reality. Fortunately, if you love God above all things, literally nothing can stop you from receiving the inheritance available to the saints now and forever. [7]

Supporting Scripture References:

1. "If anyone does not love the Lord [does not have a friendly affection for Him and is not kindly disposed toward Him], he shall be accursed! Our Lord will come! (Maranatha!)"   1 Corinthians 16:22

2. "Blessed (happy, fortunate, prosperous, and enviable) is the man who walks and lives not in the counsel of the ungodly [following their advice, their plans and purposes], nor stands [submissive and inactive] in the path where sinners walk, nor sits down [to relax and rest] where the scornful [and the mockers] gather. But his delight and desire are in the law of the Lord, and on His law (the precepts, the instructions, the teachings of God) he habitually meditates (ponders and studies) by day and by night. And he shall be like a tree firmly planted [and tended] by the streams of water, ready to bring forth its fruit in its season; its leaf also shall not fade or wither; and everything he does shall prosper [and come to maturity]."
                          Psalm 1:1-3

3. "Praise the Lord! (Hallelujah!) Blessed (happy, fortunate, to be envied) is the man who fears (reveres and worships) the Lord, who delights greatly in His commandments."
                          Psalm 112:1

4. "For I endorse and delight in the Law of God in my inmost self [with my new nature]."   Romans 7:22

5. "[Not in your own strength] for it is God Who is all the while effectually at work in you [energizing and creating in you the power and desire], both to will and to work for His good pleasure and satisfaction and delight."
                          Philippians 2:13

6. "Who were chosen and foreknown by God the Father and consecrated (sanctified, made holy) by the Spirit to be obedient to Jesus Christ (the Messiah) and to be sprinkled with [His] blood: May grace (spiritual blessing) and peace be given you in increasing abundance [that spiritual peace to be realized in and through Christ, freedom from fears, agitating passions, and moral conflicts]."   1 Peter 1:2

7. "By having the eyes of your heart flooded with light, so that you can know and understand the hope to which He has called you, and how rich is His glorious inheritance in the saints (His set-apart ones), And [so that you can know and understand] what is the immeasurable and unlimited and surpassing greatness of His power in and for us who believe, as demonstrated in the working of His mighty strength..."   Ephesians 1:18-19

Chapter Ten

The Power of Humility

Therefore humble yourselves [demote, lower yourselves in your own estimation] under the mighty hand of God, that in due time He may exalt you. . .

1 Peter 5:6

We are called to be transformed so as to resemble Christ inwardly. So let's take a look at some of the notable characteristics of Christ's heart by examining his actions. What you find are some key traits that demonstrate why He is Christ and why we are not worthy to be His brothers and sisters, even though we do accept that promise as truth.

Jesus loves the Father.

If you read about the creation of the earth and all that we perceive, it is all here as the result of the love Jesus had for His Father. In Proverbs 8:30, Jesus is described at the time of creation as, ". . . master and director of the work; and I was daily His delight, rejoicing before Him always." Jesus also repeatedly references His love and devotion to His Father. [1]

Jesus is obedient to the Father.

He says that He will only do what the Father tells Him to do and will only say what the Father tells Him to say. And that He will refuse nothing that is asked of Him by His Father. He once said, "My food (nourishment) is to do the will (pleasure) of Him who sent me. . ." John 4:34 [2]

Jesus is Forgiving.

He was able to forgive all of mankind while on the cross. He did this without first being asked by those He saved. [3]

Jesus is Humble.

He did not think so much of Himself that He felt deserving of the status of God. Instead He gave up His life and communion with His Father to visit the hell of earth and break Satan's domination. Because the Lord loved mankind, Jesus made this sacrifice for a bunch of people who did not always behave well towards His Father. [4]

Add to that limited list Jesus' power, majesty, mercy, patience, grace, and all His other characteristics. Which trait would you say best represents the core of who He is? [5]

I think it is humility, a characteristic we are all called to but usually struggle the most to exhibit. Our culture's strong tendency to reward self-glorification makes it harder to win our inner battle to walk humbly with the Lord.

The Battle for Humility

In addition to conducting prayer and healing ministry sessions with the men in the program, I have been the recipient of a similar ministry on three occasions. The ministry I participated in was designed to help those seeking general spiritual health, rather than heart level transformation or victory over addiction.

When I first heard about the process from a trusted friend, it sounded like a good idea for me, and I became very interested in getting involved as a counselor. Some months later, a training session was available at a local church, so I decided to attend.

At that time in my life, I was feeling pretty good about my relationship with the Lord, but wanted more. If that ministry would get me there, then I wanted to do it. I had been a Christian for about 15 years and was still struggling with some sin patterns I knew were wrong, but nothing I couldn't hide. My weight issue, which always presented itself as a barometer of my heart, had not been licked, although I had managed to sustain a lower weight since my first forgiveness experiences about 10 years earlier. Restored relationships from that episode had improved wonderfully, but anger continued to well up in me from time to time, and I really didn't know where to go with that. So I was doing better, but was seeking the next level.

The day of training was exciting. As the facilitator explained it, the process made good sense. I could see how the Lord might use me to set more of His people free through this ministry, and was glad to be involved. The instructional phase of the workshop lasted all morning, and the trainees were scheduled to receive ministry after lunch. I was excited, but began to feel a little anxious as I contemplated what it would mean to be the subject of focused confession and prayer time.

During the lunch hour, my anxiety grew until full-blown fear had built up inside me. By the time the afternoon sessions were to begin, I was having a "fight or flight" reaction and wanted to run screaming out of the building. I was bombarded with doubts: "What was I thinking? This is a terrible idea! I'm not doing this!"

I looked for one of the organizers to cancel my session, after which I planned to bolt. I could live without this! The person scheduling the sessions was in the middle of a roomful of people, milling around as they prepared to start. Getting his attention, I began to explain my second thoughts, but was interrupted by a wave of emotion that immediately turned to tears. All the shame and hurt of my life that still remained in my heart came out in sobs. I was deeply afraid to go into a room with a bunch of strangers, open myself up to their scrutiny, and risk revealing all my hidden sin. I had worked hard to rationalize and accommodate the sin in my heart, and I knew from the training that there would be no place to hide when it came time to confess things of which I was ashamed. The prospect was unbearable, and the emotional pain was driving me away from the thing I needed most, the opportunity to gain freedom from it all. Still, I could not stand the idea of the truth of who I was inside coming out in the session. My "I've got it together" public image, fashioned with great care and sustained with greater emotional force, appeared destined to crumble. I expected nothing short of total, stark, white-hot exposure and a humiliating end to my house-of-cards self-esteem. I stood there, all 6'3", 245 pounds of me crying like a baby, ready to run for my life.

Thankfully, a brother in Christ who had been watching the whole scene hugged me with loving compassion and prayed away my fear. God broke through the fear, allowing me to regain my composure and get my head right to receive His blessing. Later, I realized that with God's help I had won an important spiritual battle by overcoming my pride. Satan, the father of pride, had used my prideful nature to try to maintain his dark hold by stoking my fear of exposure and humiliation. But the Holy Spirit wanted the truth to set me free from the bondage of pride. With prayer, God broke through the fear and gave me enough humility to go forward with the session. He did not reward my humility with humiliation but with another break-through. [6]

The ministry session with these two men was incredible. They truly exhibited God's love for me as they patiently listened to my version of sins they had heard many times before. I felt as if I had crossed through the valley of the shadow of death, and I was hungry for the freedom this experience would yield. I wanted every bit of darkness in my life exposed. It required an avalanche of humility, and that is what God delivered. I had practically no regard for my carefully crafted image. I drove as deep as I could and was as honest as I knew how to be. Confessing, repenting, forgiving, and rebuking lies that I had accepted as truth freed me of the emotional *dis*-ease that had fueled many sinful behaviors. Thanks to God, I now had the heart to defeat them, and ultimately did. [7]

Living with Humility

Humility was essential to my success that day, just as it is essential to living a victorious life in Christ. When we are humble, we emulate the heart of Christ. Remember, it was humility that enabled Jesus to achieve victory over Satan and to forgive a people who tortured Him to death. [8]

Jesus' humility was based upon His absolute, sinless righteousness. Our humility is based on our acceptance that we are no better than anyone else. Being humble means leaving the job of our glorification to God. When we attempt self-glorification, we are trying to be God. We are fooling ourselves when we conjure up self-righteousness built on our limited goodness. Believing that we deserve praise and glory based on who we are apart from God can only lead to emotional meltdown and failure, because we are trying to assume God's role. No level of society is immune from this temptation. Seeking self-worth through the world's glory is a hopeless and self-defeating act of pride. Groveling for approval at the feet of mankind will only serve to batter our self-esteem and never truly satisfy us. Whatever corrupt and limited glory we might receive by our efforts is the world's glory. It is not the Lord's glory.[9, 10]

Self-righteousness

I had a breakthrough understanding of this concept when preparing to speak to the men in the rehab program one evening on the topic of self-righteousness. It may be hard to believe, but the men in the program struggle with self-righteousness just like the rest of us. It's not hard to imagine humility abounding in a place full of people who have been beaten down to their level. And we were impressed with the men's humility from the beginning of our experience working with them. It was good to see, knowing that it was critically important for the healing these men needed.

However, we were surprised by displays of self-righteousness in their relationships with one another. Many of the men believed they were better than some of the others and deserved some relative prominence or special consideration. It was not uncommon for these guys to stratify themselves into different levels of "goodness" based on which substances they abused or on the type of offenses they had perpetrated against others. The standard was that the less heinous the act, the better they felt as a person.

For instance, some alcoholics claimed superiority over cocaine users, who, in turn, saw themselves as being better than crack users. Child abusers were seen as worse than wife abusers. It was an elaborate system of self-righteousness that allowed the men to feel better by positioning themselves above others. It was really just another way to survive their world, which I completely understood because I had done the same thing.

I encountered self-righteousness in my heart by presuming that I was better than some people, including the guys in the program, based on the relative success of my life compared to theirs. My home-grown righteousness has always been there to make me feel more worthy and valuable. We all want to feel that we have goodness, despite God's revealed truth that says we have no righteousness in us and are totally dependent upon Jesus for salvation. Our pride just can't accept that and prods us to create some convincing case for our inherent goodness. Most commonly, we point out the mistakes of others (the ones we haven't made yet) to demonstrate our superiority. The weakness of this strategy is that we can be counted on to make one of those mistakes or something worse, and thereby nullify our brilliant rationalization, leaving us back where we started, condemned to death without Christ. [11]

The truth is that we are all a few bad decisions away from being in the same shape as the men in the program, the homeless, or the murderers on Death Row. Put under the right pressure at the right time in the right situation, I think anyone's history of good behavior can cave in. Self-righteousness is bondage that occurs when we try to build ourselves up by tearing others down. We like to think there is something special about us such that we could never make THAT mistake. We believe there is some goodness within us that could never be defiled. However, when we make that claim, it is the same as saying that we have God-like qualities. And that is exactly the deception Satan wants us to believe, because it fuels the pride that opens us up to his influence and possible fall. And it is always Satan's desire that we follow his lead by falling into his world. [6]

Humility is realizing that no matter what behavior you see demonstrated by another, you know that if you had led their life you could have easily done the same thing or something equally regretful. Humility is knowing that you are no better than anyone else – that you have no inherent goodness that makes you less dependent on God's grace or on the salvation offered through His Son.

The Blessings of Humility

Contrary to how we may feel about it, humility is a great blessing. It empowers our transformation and improves the quality of our lives now. For example, humility allows forgiveness. Forgiveness is critical to keeping our spiritual house in order. If we feel superior to others and self-righteously withhold forgiveness, we are sentenced to a life of self-destructive bitterness. As a wise man said, hating another man is like drinking poison, expecting him to die. If we feel that we are better than those who offend us, then we will resist forgiving them and give Satan a foothold to torment us. Hating someone who offends you is the same as condemning yourself to a slow death.

However, there is a more subtle aspect of humility that I didn't understand until I asked God what to say to the men that night. It is the power of humility to free us of the self-condemnation that occurs when *we* make mistakes. When it became apparent that I had been operating from a place of self-righteousness, it hit me that there is absolutely no difference between me and the drug addict who felt superior because his drug of choice was less socially unacceptable than his fellow addict's. That is really no different from how I can feel superior to someone because they had made a mistake I had not *yet* made. Considered honestly, you can only conclude that we are all on equal footing; you, me, the guys in the program and the noblest person you can think of outside of Christ. We are all beloved of the Father, we possess no inherent righteousness, and we have access to salvation through the lone road of faith in Christ.

We all make mistakes, just different ones. That is our common condition. To put it in more of a spiritual context, we have all sinned. Thus, we have no basis for

believing we possess any greater goodness or value than another, or that we have any lesser need for 100 percent of the salvation that Jesus provided through His sacrificial act.
12

What's more, as sinners we have no basis for withholding forgiveness, even if we don't receive an apology. We are called by God to pray for and bless our enemies. This does not mean after they have apologized or stopped warring against us. We are required to forgive our enemies even as they are trying to hurt or kill us.

The Humility of Christ

Consider Christ. Sinless and righteous, He did not believe Himself deserving of being God and came to this world to endure the torture of a people he had come to save. Even as He was hanging on the cross, He broke the grip of death on mankind by forgiving them of their sins. He was truly righteous, and the only being who has ever had the right to withhold forgiveness. Yet, He chose to forgive those who spit on Him in His agony. So on what basis do we withhold our forgiveness? On what basis do we condemn others? And on what basis can we proclaim ourselves better than any other person on the planet? None! [4]

Christ's actions give us insight into His heart and demonstrate the link between humility and forgiveness. Forgiveness requires humility. Humility can even keep us from being offended. Imagine if you never had to forgive anyone, not because you withheld forgiveness, but because you refused to take offense. The preemptive strike is to avoid taking offense, not by staying away from fellow sinners but by operating in the belief that those who have sinned against us have really sinned against God. It is *His* job to deal with sinners, and it is our job to avoid being offended, so that we may receive the glory due us from reflecting the heart of Christ. Remember that He did not take offense on the cross and then forgive. He took no offense for what His fellow Jews did to him. Instead, He asked the Father to forgive them. It is the same in our lives. We have no righteous justification to either take offense or withhold forgiveness. [13]

The blessing I received while seeking this understanding for the guys is that it really is okay to make mistakes. We have heard it ever since the days of our youth. We make mistakes. That is who we are, and it is okay. It doesn't mean there won't be consequences or that we won't have to make things right. But we are no better or worse than anyone else. There is no one superior to us from God's perspective.

When we pile condemnation on ourselves for making mistakes we are doing Satan's work for him. And we can generate far more internal torment than we are able to bear. I remember a time before knowing the Lord when I made an embarrassing public mistake. You could have sent Satan on a holiday, because I beat myself up for a week with no assistance required from him. My fragile self-esteem, which was built on my fragile sense of self-worth, which was housed in my "mistakes I will never make" glass house all came crashing down. As a result of the ensuing torment of condemnation, I spent the rest of the week trying to separate myself from the negative feelings by relying on familiar bad choices. Nope, Satan was not required. I did just fine executing a perfect nose dive into gloom.

It was seeking the Lord's answer for the guys' struggle with self-righteousness that exposed me to the truth about humility. Many of the men I counseled were suffering from the weight of self-condemnation served up by their self-righteousness, just as I had so many times in the past. As I described in the "Breakthrough" chapter, it was an epiphany to experience the absence of self-condemnation after a public failing. It is hard to say how the guys were affected by my message that night, but a big chunk of my self-righteousness was removed when I accepted the truth and repented.

All of us on the landscape of humanity have sin and imperfection in common. We can experience freedom in that equality if we let the transforming truth sink into our hearts, so that we are able to freely forgive ourselves and others. We can also choose not to take offense. These actions would honor God, bless us, and be consistent with His call to be transformed into His image.

Supporting Scripture References:

1. "In the beginning [before all time] was the Word (Christ), and the Word was with God, and the Word was God Himself. He was present originally with God. All things were made and came into existence through Him; and without Him was not even one thing made that has come into being. In Him was Life, and the Life was the Light of men."   John 1:1-4

2. "For I have come down from heaven not to do My own will and purpose but to do the will and purpose of Him Who sent Me."   John 6:38

3. "And Jesus prayed, Father, forgive them, for they know not what they do. And they divided His garments and distributed them by casting lots for them."   Luke 23:34

4. "Let this same attitude and purpose and [humble] mind be in you which was in Christ Jesus: [Let Him be your example in humility:] Who, although being essentially one with God and in the form of God [possessing the fullness of the attributes which make God God], did not think this equality with God was a thing to be eagerly grasped or retained, But stripped Himself [of all privileges and rightful dignity], so as to assume the guise of a servant (slave), in that He became like men and was born a human being. And after He had appeared in human form, He abased and humbled Himself [still further] and carried His obedience to the extreme of death, even the death of the cross!"
                    Philippians 2:5-8

5. "[Now] He is the exact likeness of the unseen God [the visible representation of the invisible]; He is the Firstborn of all creation. For it was in Him that all things were created, in heaven and on earth, things seen and things

unseen, whether thrones, dominions, rulers, or authorities; all things were created and exist through Him [by His service, intervention] and in and for Him. And He Himself existed before all things, and in Him all things consist (cohere, are held together). He also is the Head of [His] body, the church; seeing He is the Beginning, the Firstborn from among the dead, so that He alone in everything and in every respect might occupy the chief place [stand first and be preeminent]."   Colossians 1:15-18

6. "Pride goes before destruction, and a haughty spirit before a fall."   Proverbs 16:18

7. "Confess to one another therefore your faults (your slips, your false steps, your offenses, your sins) and pray [also] for one another, that you may be healed and restored [to a spiritual tone of mind and heart]. The earnest (heartfelt, continued) prayer of a righteous man makes tremendous power available [dynamic in its working]."   James 5:16

8. "Let each of you esteem and look upon and be concerned for not [merely] his own interests, but also each for the interests of others. Let this same attitude and purpose and [humble] mind be in you which was in Christ Jesus: [Let Him be your example in humility:]" Philippians 2:4-5

9. "Humble yourselves [feeling very insignificant] in the presence of the Lord, and He will exalt you [He will lift you up and make your lives significant]."   James 4:10

10. "Jesus answered, If I were to glorify Myself (magnify, praise, and honor Myself), I would have no real glory, for My glory would be nothing and worthless. [My honor must come to Me from My Father.] It is My Father Who glorifies Me [Who extols Me, magnifies, and praises Me], of Whom you say that He is your God."   John 8:54

11."For we have all become like one who is unclean [cere-
monially, like a leper], and all our righteousness (our best
deeds of rightness and justice) is like filthy rags or a pol-
luted garment; we all fade like a leaf, and our iniquities, like
the wind, take us away [far from God's favor, hurrying us
toward destruction]."   Isaiah 64:6

12. "Since all have sinned and are falling short of the honor
and glory which God bestows and receives. [All] are justified and made upright and in right standing with God,
freely and gratuitously by His grace (His unmerited favor
and mercy), through the redemption which is [provided] in
Christ Jesus..."   Romans 3:23-24

13. "Good sense makes a man restrain his anger, and it is
his glory to overlook a transgression or an offense."
                                                    Proverbs 19:11

Chapter Eleven

Let the Transformation Begin

And just as we have borne the image [of the man] of dust, so shall we and so let us also bear the image [of the Man] of heaven.
1 Corinthians 15:49

One thing I observed during my first 22 years as a Christian is that most believers want a change. They want to be somewhere other than where they are spiritually, emotionally, or physically. The rehab guys, who were all professing Christians, want to be free of their addiction. Obese Christians want to be thin. People in bad relationships want happiness. Converted criminals want their lives turned around. And legions of believers want a more fulfilling faith. I doubt I've ever met a believer who didn't want some life improvement or at least some richer faith experience. It is certainly the way I feel now and have felt all along my transformation continuum. Could it be we are all feeling a universal urge that was sown into our being when God made us in His image? Do we have a holy discontent that only His transformation working in us can satisfy?

Have you ever considered the message inherent in

the New Testament structure? First are the Gospels that largely deal with how Christ saved us by breaking sin's death grip. The Book of Acts focuses on the Spirit-filled work of the disciples. And the apostles' letters are concerned with understanding and obeying God's Law. The New Testament, apart from Revelation, could be roughly summarized as writings on faith, acts and obedience. We would not be Christians without faith. We seem to do pretty well with all kinds of helpful acts that are at least credited to God. Obedience is really where we seem to fall short, and the consequences of those shortcomings largely account for our suffering.

Obeying God means living by His laws, which are perfectly designed to usher in our transformation. Regardless of what we want to believe, transformation is the only way to satisfy our common desire to move out of our current life situation and into more of His abundant life. When our hearts resemble Christ's, we will share in His divine nature. The only way to find the life we seek is to begin pursuing a new life, and that means dying to who we are today. The good news is that each incremental step we take toward transformation brings rewards that encourage us to reach for the next breakthrough.

Remember the chapter on humility? It explains that humility is the essence of the heart of Christ and the trait that enabled Him to accomplish His powerful work. Humility is also what opens our hearts for God to do His work in us. To jumpstart your transformation, make a commitment to discern with humility the truth about who you are and to submit humbly to His laws.

Here's how to open your heart for God's transformation:

1. Decide that you will not attempt life change based on superficial behavior modification. Instead, decide you

want your heart rewired by God. Seek to have a new life at peace with a new heart. No quick fixes allowed!

Prayer of Commitment

Heavenly Father, I confess that my life is not what You want for me. I commit to humbly confront any part of my life that is required to open my heart to Your transformation. I reject the lie that a quick fix solution is the answer. I want a new life, not just a new appearance. Thank You for loving me and being willing to do the transforming work. I commit to give up those things in my life that keep me from being transformed into the likeness of Your Son. I ask for You to give me strength to stay on Your path of transformation. I pray these things in the name of Jesus. Amen.

2.   Remove the torment from your life by repenting for breaking God's laws and deciding to conform to them from now on. Forgive those people who have caused you pain. Practice humility – it will help you side-step the self-righteousness that tempts us to withhold forgiveness.

Prayer for Guidance

Heavenly Father, forgive me for the times in my life when I have not conformed to Your laws. I repent of those actions and desire to conform my heart to Your laws. Father please reveal to me who I need to forgive or any of Your laws I live in opposition to. I ask these things in the name of Jesus. Amen.

Forgiveness Prayer

Heavenly Father, I forgive [Name]. I forgive [him or her] for: [list everything you can think of that caused the offense]. I ask that You forgive [Name] as well. Father, please bless [Name]'s life in every way and heal [Name] of any emotional or physical wounds that cause [Name] suffering. [If you are not sure of person's salvation in Christ:] Lord, I also pray for [Name]'s salvation and ask that You would write [Name]'s name in the Book of Life and compel [Name] to seek Your salvation. [If the person is deceased:] Father, it is the desire of my heart for You to bless [Name] even in death. I ask these things in the name of Jesus. Amen.

3. Ask God to forgive you for trying to soothe your pain with the world's solutions instead of God's. Genuine repentance will help you turn away from the world.

Prayer to Repent of Faith in Idols

Heavenly Father, I ask Your forgiveness for seeking worldly solutions for my troubled soul instead of turning to You. In the name of Jesus, I rebuke the lie that the world can fill my heart with lasting peace and joy. Specifically I ask Your forgiveness for turning to [Name the sin, e.g. alcohol, pornography, cocaine, gossip, gluttony, etc. If more than one, pray for forgiveness for each one separately.] instead of to You for the answer to my torment. I ask You to guide me in the process of building a new life that is dependent on You instead of on my past medicating behavior. I ask these things in the name of Jesus. Amen.

4. Rebuke any statements made about you that conflict with who God says you are. If somebody has told you that you are a "nobody," it is a lie because you are a child of God. If you were the only person on this earth, Jesus would still have sacrificed His life to save you. If someone says

you are ugly, that is a lie because you are made in the glorious image of God. If someone has said you are stupid, that is a lie because you have the Holy Spirit, which is the mind of God, within you. Many of us have lived under lies that have been spoken over us. Forgive the people who have said those things and repent of having believed them. You are to live under the truth of who God says you are.

Prayer to Substitute Truth for Lies

Heavenly Father, I forgive any person who has spoken lies over me. I ask that You would forgive them, bless them, and help them come to know how much You love them. Father forgive me for believing anything that opposes Your truth. I reject and rebuke those lies in the name of Jesus. I specifically rebuke the lie that [description from lie column below] and proclaim Your Truth that [description from truth column. Continue through the list as it applies to your life. Add more as needed.]

LIE	TRUTH
I am worthless.	I was chosen by God before the beginning of time. Galatians. 1:13 Ephesians. 1:5
I am stupid.	I have the Holy Spirit dwelling in me which knows the mind of God. Romans 8:27 Knowing God is the beginning of all wisdom Psalm 111:10.

I am ugly.	I am made in the image of God. Genesis 1:27
I am a loser.	All things work to good for me because I love God and I am called according to His purposes. Romans 8:28
I am unlovable.	I am loved perfectly by the Creator of the universe. John 15:9 Romans 1:20
I am unworthy.	I am so important to Jesus that He would have sacrificed Himself for me if I had been the only one in the entire universe to save. John 15:13,14
I am evil.	I have been given a new nature which desires good. Ephesians 4:24
I am undesirable.	I have been chosen to be the brother (or sister) of Christ and rule with Him for eternity. Romans 8:29, 1 Corinthians 6:3
I'm a hopeless sinner.	I have been made righteous in the sight of God by the

death and resurrection of
His Son, Jesus Christ and
my faith in Him.
I Peter 3:12,18

5. Live a life that is devoted to God. Avoid sin. The
Bible doesn't specifically state that you will be turned over
to the tormentor for *every* sin. There are, however, negative
consequences for every sin, not the least of which is that
sin grieves the Holy Spirit and alienates us from God. The
good news is that God is ready to forgive sins like lusting,
stealing, adultery, sex outside of marriage and more when
you repent and align your heart with His. For a quick
refresher on how God defines a Christian life, check out
the gospel of Matthew, chapters six and seven.

Prayer to Repent of Specific Sin

Heavenly Father, forgive me for my sins. Specifically forgive me for [name the sin] and for hurting
all those who were harmed by my actions. I recognize that my sin grieves the Holy Spirit and makes it
hard for me to hear His gentle voice. For that I am
truly sorry. Please give me a heart that treasures
Your presence and leadership above all things. I ask
this in the name of Jesus. Amen.

6. Love God more than anything in your life. If you
just do this, a transformed heart and life is assured. If you
love a sin, you are crowding God out of your heart. The
Holy Spirit yearns to be accepted and loved. You may have
fallen in love with a self-destructive behavior. You may also
love things like peer approval, winning, or your job, but
they must all be demoted below God. The only pure thing
we can love and put our hope in is God. He will not disap-
point us. Everything else has the potential for bondage and

disappointment. You must love Him more than anything.

This has been revealed to me over the years as I tried to claim the benefits of a new life without giving up the old. While this truth was apparent in ministries I was involved in related to marriage, youth, music, and parenting, it was through my ministry in the rehab program that I saw the truth by heartbreaking example. Time after time, men seeking treatment for addiction were unable to break free because they were only willing to change their religious routines. They naively believed that new routines would be enough to help them maintain their hard-won sobriety. They were wrong. Had they taken away from their time in drug rehab a new heart that loved God more than their drug of choice, the outcomes would have been very different.

Prayer to Rebuke Idols and Love God More

Heavenly Father, forgive me for loving anything more than I love You. Specifically forgive me for idolizing [name your idol, e.g. food, drugs, work, money pornography, etc. Pray about each idol separately.] I rebuke the idol and proclaim my love for You above all else. Give me a heart that loves You above all things and the strength to change my life to demonstrate that love. I ask this in the name of Jesus. Amen.

7. Fight self-righteousness with humility. Pride is one of the greatest stumbling blocks to transformation. It will remove you from the presence of God just as it did Satan. The opposite of Christ, Satan was an angel so full of pride he aspired to God's position. Upon his fall, he became the accuser of man. He was the most beautiful and charismatic angel, but he believed he had inherent goodness by his actions rather than by God's grace. You must accept that

you have no righteousness without Jesus and credit God for your gifts and good fortune. When you operate from a position of humility, God will send reward and glory into your life.

Prayer of Humility

Heavenly Father, forgive me for ever believing that I have any goodness or righteousness in me. Forgive me for not giving You credit for my gifts and position in life. I proclaim that You are responsible for all the goodness in my life and for that I praise You. Father, forgive me for trying to glorify myself. I proclaim that only the glory of Your making will truly lift me up. Give me the gift of humility and the strength to stop seeking the approval of man. I ask this in the name of Jesus. Amen.

8. Reject everything in your life that supports undesirable lifestyles or behaviors. Diligently build a new life that supports the new person God wants you to be. This new life could mean changing your home, neighborhood, friends, hobbies, conversations, clothes, or job. It could really mean virtually anything. There should be nothing that you are unwilling to change if you want to be free of the old self and its undesirable ways. I was moved to give up most movies because they were drawing me back to the old me. If you love movies, this may sound extreme. But there are many things we do, mostly unaware, that feed the part of us that needs to go.

While it may be hard to consider removing certain things from your life, understand that you are just plain stuck if you are not willing to give up whatever it takes to be transformed. The change may be hard if you have become dependent on a sinful behavior to medicate tormenting feelings. You may feel you have the right to do whatever you want as long as it doesn't hurt anyone else. That would be confusing the Bible with the Bill of Rights. Remember that what is spiritually damaging for you also hurts the people around you. Giving up some or all of the things and activities you love will be necessary for transformation. Remember that a payoff will come in the quality of your new life.

Prayer of Commitment to a New Life

Heavenly Father, please forgive me for holding on to anything that stands in the way of You transforming my heart. I proclaim in the name of Jesus that there is nothing in my life that I refuse to give up to have a heart that reflects the heart of Your Son Jesus. Father, I ask that You give me the strength to abandon for a time or forever any part of my life that is not consistent with Your will. I also ask for Your help in identifying those things about my life that must be addressed to accomplish the heart change that we both want for me. I ask these things in the name of Jesus. Amen.

Well, there you have it! I am done! I guess this would be the time to tell you I am not a writer and have never had any real desire to try my hand at it. This book was written with two purposes: First, to communicate to you my understanding of God's call to all followers of Christ to be transformed; and, second, to tell you that you _can_ attain the life you want in the innermost part of who you are. In this life, the temptation of sin can be reduced to an annoyance from something that can control and destroy your life. In the next life, we can look forward to total freedom from the sin nature.

Until I began writing this book, I was feeling a constant internal pressure to get this message off my chest. A book seemed to be a good way to pass on my understanding, but my schedule was so hectic that I never got around to it. Then, in December of 2005, I experienced a lull in my business and decided it was time to sit down and write until I was done. Six weeks later the first draft of this book was complete.

I also wrote this book because I want you, no matter who you are or where you are in your faith journey, to have the heart God wants for you. A new heart will bring you a life that is incomparably better than anything you could cobble together from the world's offerings. I urge you to align your heart with His and receive the life that the deepest part of you hungers for and won't be satisfied without.